Engaging Angels
in the Realms of Heaven

Opening the Door to the Angelic Realm

by

Dr. Ron M. Horner

Engaging Angels
in the Realms of Heaven

Opening the Door to the Angelic Realm

By

Dr. Ron M. Horner

www.CourtsOfHeaven.Net
PO Box 2167
Albemarle, North Carolina 28002

Engaging Angels in the Realms of Heaven

Opening the Door to the Angelic Realm

Copyright © 2020 Dr. Ron M. Horner

Scripture is taken from the New King James Version®. Copyright © 1982 by Thomas Nelson. Used by permission. All rights reserved. (Unless otherwise noted.)

Scripture quotations marked (MIRROR) are taken from THE MIRROR. Copyright ©2012. Used by permission of The Author.

Any copyrights or trademarks mentioned are the property of their respective owners.

All rights reserved. This book is protected by the copyright laws of the United States of America. This book may not be copied or reprinted for commercial gain or profit. The use of short quotations or occasional page copying for personal or group study is permitted and encouraged. Permission will be granted upon request.

Requests for bulk sales discounts, editorial permissions, or other information should be addressed to:

LifeSpring Publishing
PO Box 2167
Albemarle, NC 28002 USA
www.lifespringpublishing.com

Additional copies available at www.courtsofheaven.net

ISBN 13 TP: 978-1-953684-02-8
ISBN 13 eBook: 978-1-953684-03-5

Cover Design by Darian Horner Design
(www.darianhorner.com)
Images: stock.adobe.com #86383061, #241753603, #31707414

First Edition: December 2020

10 9 8 7 6 5 4 3 2 1

Printed in the United States of America

Table of Contents

Acknowledgements i
Foreword iii
Preface vii
Chapter 1 Heaven Has Been Waiting 1
Chapter 2 Guardian Angels vs Personal Angels 7
Chapter 3 Understanding Angels 19
Chapter 4 Guardians & Their Realms 23
Chapter 5 How to Work with Your Angel Part 1 39
Chapter 6 How to Work with Your Angel Part 2 49
Chapter 7 Angels in Captivity 71
Chapter 8 Angels & Relationships 83
Chapter 9 Messenger Angels 89
Chapter 10 Cooperating with
the Angel of Currency 103
Chapter 11 Court of Decrees
and the Court of Angels 107
Chapter 12 Plundering the Enemies Camp 115
Chapter 13 Working with Bond Registry Angels 121
Chapter 14 Communication Pathways 127
Chapter 15 Timed Devices 135

Chapter 16 Angelic Perceptions 141
Chapter 17 Court of Accounting 143
Chapter 18 Insights 157
Chapter 19 Conclusion 171
Appendix A 173
Accessing the Realms of Heaven 173
Learning to Live Spirit First 181
Four Keys to Hearing God's Voice 189
Appendix B 191
Index of Types of Angels 191
Index of Courts Mentioned 193
Description 195
About the Author 197
Other Books by Dr. Ron M. Horner 199

Acknowledgements

Acknowledging all that were essential help in the creation of this book would include those alive on the earth and those who have already accessed Heaven on a permanent basis. It would include men and women in white as well as many angels as well as many other sources.

Donna Neeper has been willing to pioneer in our frequent engagements with Heaven and I am grateful for her assistance. My wife Adina and daughters Darian and Bethany have played an active role as well. To our CourtsNet students and the family of our Courts of Heaven Mentoring Group – thank you. And to those I may have failed to mention – thank you. May the blessing of the Lord be rich upon you.

Foreword

This book is a crucible that will test out the maturity of the Bride and now is the time for the Bride to understand her ability to engage Heaven, to interact with the angels of God, and to operate out of her right to access Heaven in this hour. This book is a door to understanding. It is the invitation to gain understanding of angelic realms and the activity of unseen angels.

The Bride is right on the cusp of receiving a whole new understanding that is being birthed. Revelation is being released about the ability of the Bride to engage angels and to co-labor with them in their angelic assignments. This unseen realm is going to break into the seen realm with greater frequency; and those who have even a grain of faith will be touched by these visitations.

Do you remember Abraham meeting with the visitors sent from the Father? Get ready in future days for the visitation of angelic beings who will, at the assignment of the Father, release themselves to be seen. This happens more frequently than we know. It is about to delight this next generation. They are the generation chosen to begin to explore the power of God's hosts, and to discover the safety that God provides to his believers through the angelic.

This book contains an impartation to those who believe in their heart and are reading this book with the expectation that their thought patterns and their essence—the lifeblood within—will shift as a result. A shift will come that is connected to the indwelling of the Holy Spirit. As you read, allow yourself to be shifted forward in momentum, to understand the beauty of the hosts of Heaven and the glory of what they are created for. Receive their help and their work. Praise the Lord for them and thank them for their activity.

Remember, it is okay to know in part because that is what it feels like to the soul. The soul clamors for complete knowledge of all things, but some of these things are hidden in God, and through the Spirit indwelling your spirit, you begin to have a greater glimmer of understanding and more clarity. Seeing in part is okay. Give yourself permission to see in part. Go with what you do see. Go with what you know.

As you read this book, recall the Spirit of the Lord, the Spirit of His Glory, the Spirit who is your instructor, who is your teacher, the Spirit who is the most beautiful of all. The guidance, teaching, instruction, and help He can provide for you while you read this book is beyond amazing. Let me encourage you to agree with Him verbally as you set out to read this book. Ask that the Spirit of Counsel come and read this book along with you.

This book also contains an impartation to write about your experiences regarding the angelic in blog posts, articles, journals, and books. Share what you experience as you read and put into practice the information that you learn in this book.

The human race is being stirred up to recognize the potential for dealing with the unseen realm. A key from Heaven has been released to unlock your heart, and the heart of those who do not yet know the Savior to awaken the desire to engage with the unseen realm. Do you receive this key?

A banner has also been released over this book declaring "Glory to Him in Whom All Things Are." Heaven has been petitioned that an ocean wave of the Glory of God would be released to flood the land with what the human race thirsts for—what it hungers for. Ron has asked for the power of the wave of Yahweh to come and fill up all that is lacking in this book with Holy Spirit.

Do not read this book alone. Ron has requested the presence of the Lampstand of the Father—the Spirit of Counsel to be present in the heart of every reader, in the mind of every reader, in you as you read these things. Receive the gift of the Lampstand from the Father. May God's glory be revealed by the reading of this.

Lydia

Preface

The misinformation concerning angels is immense, not merely in the Body of Christ, but throughout the earth. We have been taught that angels are frail, dainty, cupid-like creatures that have little power and that we are subordinate to them. That is not the case.

The angels illustrated in the Bible are mighty and powerful, with great strength to defeat our enemies. They appear throughout scripture to subdue kings and kingdoms, to bring messages of hope, and to save lives. Hebrews refers to them as ministers to those who are heirs of salvation.[1] The psalmist recorded that they were flames of fire.[2] The angels of scripture are hardly cupid-like figures.

We have also been taught erroneously that when someone dies, it was because God needed another angel. This implies that we, especially babies and young children, become angels upon passing from this realm. This teaching is inaccurate! We are a different class of

---

[1] Hebrews 1:14 Are they not all ministering spirits sent forth to minister for those who will inherit salvation?
[2] Psalms 104:4 Who makes His angels spirits, His ministers a flame of fire.

beings, and angels are subordinate to our position in the hierarchy of Heaven.

We have been taught to be afraid of angels because they stand ready to strike us down if we sin. The Bible does have a story or two where angels dealt serious damage to unruly humans, but those were rare exceptions. Angels are here to help us expand the Kingdom of God. If you realize that you have been afraid of angels, repent of embracing fear and ask Holy Spirit to completely erase it from your being with the Sword of the Spirit.

The human race, in the providence of God, was singled out among all other created beings to be the recipients of the grace of God—to bring redemption to mankind through the blood of Jesus Christ shed on the cross for our salvation. Humans were chosen for that opportunity; no other class of being was selected for such a high honor. Angels were not given that honor. Angels are a class of being that God designed for service—they serve God, and they serve us. We are given the opportunity to co-labor with angels to achieve Kingdom purposes.

Unfortunately for us, we have little understood their role, their races, their ranking, and their purposes; and it has cost us dearly. In the pages of this book, we are going to unlock understandings Heaven has granted to us concerning these heavenly servants, and how we can engage with them for the expansion of the Kingdom of God. You will be reading of our engagements with angels, men, and women in white linen, and with Holy Spirit, as well as with other beings in Heaven. If you have read some of my other books, you will find the format familiar.

Nowhere are we worshipping angels. Nor are we ignoring the value of what they know, do, and possess. Many of us have been taught to fear them. We will address that subject and how to be free of the fear so you can more fully cooperate with these messengers from Heaven. Neither will this book be a treatise on the many verses in the Bible on angels (nearly 300). Simply suffice it to say, that the early translators often misinterpreted many passages related to angels and their work and we have suffered for it.

Let me encourage you concerning your partnership with angels and other voices in the earth realm now currently writing about angels, namely Barbie Breathitt, Kevin Zadai, Tim Sheets, and many others. Many are writing about angels, partnership with angels, and the Father's release of revelation regarding angelic activity in the earth realm. I want to encourage you to read other books to round out your knowledge and depth regarding this topic.

It is okay to feel elementary in the understanding of angels at this point but as you press in (just as you pressed into the understanding of dreams in a bygone era) so the pressing into the understanding of the angelic realm is going to grow and your experience with and knowledge of angels both spiritually and physically is going to increase. Angels are desirous of your increased knowledge and understanding of them and how they love what the Father has loved and how they are created to love what the Father has loved.

May this book and these coming pages open you to new understandings and bring encouragement to know your Personal Angel and begin engaging with them as a daily exercise. Your life will never be the same if you choose to do so.

Take a moment before you go any further prepare ourselves to receive the revelation in this book. It is important to have our soul step back and our spirit come to the forefront.

We refer to this as living spirit first. For most of us, we have lived with our soul in charge of our daily affairs and we have not allowed our spirit to have much input into our daily lives. That is not how we are to live. The apostle Paul instructed us over and over to live in the spirit. This is what he was referring to. Now, speak aloud to your soul and instruct it to step back. Then, speak to your spirit and instruct it to come forward. Did you feel that shift?

Learning to live spirit forward is essential for our spiritual growth so that our spirit can become the dominant force in our lives. As this book is packed with revelation and revelatory insights, it is essential that we glean from this book through our spirit, as opposed to our intellect. It is not written to appeal to your intellect.

It is written to appeal to your spirit, which yearns for more information from Heaven whence it came. Your spirit has been yearning for revelatory insights from Heaven ever since your conception. If you are fifty, your soul has had a fifty-year head start. We must change our approach and be spirit-led, as opposed to soul-led. You can do it. It will simply require some practice on your part and the decision to read this book from your spirit as opposed to your natural mind.

Some things will not make sense at first, but as your spirit can assist your soul in the processing of the information, understanding will come. To help with this process, pause right now and speak to your soul, "Soul, you will cooperate with my spirit and with Holy Spirit as you read this book. You will not dominate, but rather you will be subordinate to my spirit and to Holy Spirit." Now, speak to your spirit saying, "Spirit, I commission you to begin helping my soul process and accept what witnesses from my spirit with Holy Spirit. I give you permission to be the dominant voice in my life, in Jesus' name."

Now, begin to pray in the spirit for a few moments until you sense your spirit is in position and has begun to minister to your soul.

This approach will allow you to glean the maximum amount from your time with this book. Whenever you sense your soul struggling and wanting to regain pre-imminence, simply pause, speak to your soul, and tell it to calm down. Reassure it that things will be OK. Holy

Spirit is in charge. Now, step into the realms of Heaven and begin to receive.[3]

As you read this book, at times you will be reading our dialogue with Lydia, a woman in white who advises our ministry, or Ezekiel, the chief angel over our ministry. Others aided us as well. However, simply personalize what you read of our experience to your own experiences. It is our hope that the revelations and experiences recorded in this book will help catapult you in your understanding and engagement of angels and with the realms of Heaven. Have fun!

---

[3] I speak more of this in the Appendix under *Learning to Live Spirit First*.

Chapter 1

Heaven Has Been Waiting

Heaven has been waiting a long time for this era in history. The sons of men are becoming sons of God in new and exciting fashions. They are learning to live by their spirit and follow the revelatory flow of Heaven. They are learning to engage with Heaven, the men and women in white linen, the angels, and the living creatures the Bible mentions, but does not often describe. Perhaps we would find it too unbelievable. Our culture has sought to define us and to define God for us, however, the problem of that has existed from the time of Adam in the Garden of Eden. He colluded with Eve to eat of the Tree of the Knowledge of Good and Evil and we have been dealing with the consequences of that meal ever since.

Although the Father was not taken by surprise by, Adam's actions they certainly were not the best choice he could have made. We have done similarly in our lives so we cannot complain too loudly. Yet now we are in a time when we are learning new things about Heaven, about how to access it, and how to engage with Heaven in dimensions that were unheard of just a few years ago. Society has sought to insult believers engaging with Heaven by calling them mystics, but the definition of a mystic is simple. Mystic means one who knows God. That does not sound like a bad thing to me. How about you?

You may have heard someone mockingly say of someone who always seemed to be thinking and talking about heavenly things, "they are so heavenly minded they are no earthly good." I like what a friend says, "I want to be so heavenly minded that I am earthly incredible!"

In Colossians 3:1-3 we read:

If then you were raised with Christ, seek those things which are above, where Christ is, sitting at the right hand of God. ² Set your mind on things above, not on things on the earth. ³ For you died, and your life is hidden with Christ in God.

If we have said things like the mockers that I just mentioned, we need to repent because Colossians 3:1-3 clearly instructs us to think on Heaven and live out of Heaven. The Mirror Translation of this passage reads:

¹ See yourselves co-raised with Christ! Now ponder with persuasion the consequence of your co-inclusion in him. Relocate yourselves mentally! Engage your thoughts with throne room realities where you are co-seated with Christ in the executive authority of God's right hand. ² Becoming affectionately acquainted with throne room thoughts will keep you from being distracted again by the earthly [soul-ruled] realm. ³ Your union with his death broke the association with that world; see yourselves located in a fortress where your life is hidden with Christ in God! (MIRROR)

We must be willing to engage Heaven on entirely new dimensions that we may never have considered before. That engagement must also include our willingness to engage the angelic realm. Not only our Personal Angels, but other angels from that realm as well.

When studying the subject of angels (or "angelology") we find a great many gaps in scripture. Heaven must fill those gaps for us. The great news is Heaven is willing to do so. Throughout this book you will read of engagements with Heaven and of revelation released to us as we sought the Father and His Kingdom.

One of the most common things we hear when discussing angels with people is the fact, they want to know their angel's name. Heaven has made several means available. In Chapter 5, you can read Donna's story about that; however, let me begin with some basics to help you past this issue. Those who will engage the realities of Heaven without doubt will experience amazing revelatory encounters.

---

*This is the era
of revelatory encounters!*

It is not essential that you know your angel's name. It is helpful and will probably assist you in your engagement with your angel, but if you do not yet know your angel's name it does not disqualify you from engaging them. Challenges in learning their name(s) may simply be a part of our journey and become part of your testimony of engagement.

Unveiled in a Dream

Often Heaven will introduce you to your angel in a dream. You may not be able to see the face of the person in the dream, which is a clue that this may be your angel. In the dream, the person (or animal—often a horse) has characteristics that you would associate with an angel. Pay attention to your dream and if you think you have had a dream unveiling your angel to you, but you missed it at the time of the dream, ask Heaven for a second chance. Pay close attention in your dreams.

Engaging by Choice

In any event, everything we do concerning Heaven we do by faith. We can begin to engage with our angel simply by choice. We can begin to converse with them, give them instructions, commissions, etc. You may ask their advice or input on a matter and they may assist you or counsel you in a thing. That happened quite often in the writing of this book, as you will read shortly.

Journaling with Heaven

We can simply ask of Heaven and listen for Heaven to speak. It may come as an impression to your spirit, or you may hear it or see it. If you know how to do spirit-led journaling as we teach, then journal with Heaven about this information. Heaven wants you to know. Heaven does not want interaction with Heaven to be an eternal mystery to you.[4]

Court of Angels

Another option is to access the Court of Angels and request to know your angel's name from that court. They have records of every angel and can assist you. Again, pay attention to what you hear or sense, and do not second guess. Be sure you have instructed your soul to step back and you have called your spirit to come forward prior to doing these things.

Enlisting a Seer

You may request someone you know, who is a strong seer, to assist you. Often, they can help you determine this information.

Again, realize that Heaven wants you to gain access to this information, but do not get discouraged. Keep pressing in. You will likely sense them before you see

---

[4] I speak more of this in the Appendix under *Four Keys to Hearing God's Voice.*

them. The chapters on *How to Work with Your Angel* will help you if you are having difficulty.

Remember to call your spirit forward and instruct your soul to relax and rest while you read and ingest the material in this book. Allow Holy Spirit to help you process the revelations you are about to receive. Remember, He will guide you into all truth.

Chapter 2

Guardian Angels vs Personal Angels

Having heard the term Guardian Angel multiple times in my life, I wondered what (if any) difference existed between a Guardian Angel and a Personal Angel. So, Heaven responded with an answer.

"The Guardian Angel has oversight over the young, and a Guardian Angel is meant to become the Personal Angel of the individual. Guardian Angels are assigned by the love of the Father for his creation because He knows that we need protection, just as we protect our children when they are young. The Father protects his young with the assistance of Guardian Angels who protect them in numerous ways—physical, mental, and spiritual. At the coming of age where a child having been instructed that God exists, begins to recognize that for themselves and begins to sense the drawing of Holy Spirit to receive sonship through the Redeemer's blood, His body, and His name. The coalescence of this results in a change of the

Guardian Angel to the status of a Personal Angel," Ezekiel explained.

"Do angels have what we would consider a growing up and maturing?" we asked.

"It is more a ranking where they morph through what we would call physical changes due to the ranking assigned and granted to them. Their appearance may mature just as a humans' appearance changes over time. It is not a maturing as we would think of it, however they can grow in ranking," Ezekiel noted.

"When are Angels given their assignment to a person to become their Guardian Angel?" we inquired.

"It has been long planned. Upon the agreement of one to live out their scroll at the appointed time, an angel or angels are assigned to that scroll awaiting the coming to earth of the human. Their assignment is both to the scroll and to the individual. Upon conception, the angel is called into duty to minister and protect the human—particularly regarding protecting their spirit. Their soul is yet to be truly formed but is in process and, of course, their human frame is in formation as well; however, their spirit is fully functioning from the moment of conception," Ezekiel described.

Classifications of Angels

All angels yearn for their highest rank of achievement that is bestowed. Nevertheless, there are different classifications of angels and these classifications are firm. Angels do not transfer from classification to classification or class to class,[5] however they can transform from rank to rank. Just like growing up, you do not change into a giraffe as you grow up because that is a different class. So, angels stay in their class, but they do move through a ranking of achievement and increase in oversight.

Angels are Realms

Angels *have* realms and angels *are* realms as well. All angels have realms. Think in terms of a dimensional space. They are not fixed realms, they are malleable.

For instance, certain angels are assigned by the Father for specific assignments. Their classification is different from what we shared about Guardian Angels, Personal Angels, or angels assigned to work with you. Some angels are not assigned to work with you, rather they are assigned to bring about the will of the Father. It is a type of angel. This is what they do.

A massive number of angels exist who are meant to co-labor with the living in the earth realm. These are angels that are often bored if the spiritual side of a person is veiled, diminished, never investigated, considered, or regarded, or they never engage their angel.

---

[5] i.e. Gathering Angels remain Gathering Angels, Messenger Angels remain Messenger Angels although they may increase in rank.

Then you have fallen angels, which is a whole other book. Just like just like we would work with our Personal Angel or Ezekiel as the ministry angel, evil people work with spiritual beings once known as angels. They collude with them. They collaborate with them. They make promises one to another that they cannot keep. The reason they cannot keep them is they all fall under the jurisdiction of Yahweh, who will not allow the promises to be kept. Nevertheless, they are getting away with it at times due to the lack of knowledge in the saints, the adjudication of the angelic, and the stewarding of the realms that have been released to people by the Father.

Can you see why revelation is so primary? To live by revelation is to live as a son of God. Remember the revelation of "All things begin in the spirit"? All things do and have begun in the spirit, and I am speaking of ALL THINGS—all is all! Once we accept that all things begin in the spirit, we need to determine if it has begun in the spirit of darkness or in the spirit of light.

This discernment is important, and your discernment of revelation will be affected by where you choose to focus—whether you are focused on the Father's light and Glory and Kingdom, or whether you are focused on a defeated foe. You need to consider where most of your time is spent focusing, because your focus affects what you are receiving.

The enemy overall seeks to keep many veiled to their spiritual nature and if not veiled—completely unaware. Then he brings in misleading lies, negative things, traumatic pain, and the like to capture the spiritual nature. He is after both spirit and soul.

> *The easiest thing for Satan to do is to capture your body.*

Satan is hoping that through your flesh, he will rule over you, so that your soul is open to him. Once he rules over the soul, the spirit follows. That wicked way is not the plan of the Father, nor is this what Jesus introduced as the overwhelming victorious plan of the Father. All things have been made open for those who will find and follow the Father by stepping into the realms of Heaven receiving full access from their spirit for a full awakening in their spirit, soul, and body.

All three of your realms—spirit, soul, and body—will respond to the Father's light. That is the importance of focusing on who He is, where He is, what He is, and how He is. Learning how Father is—His nature, character, and design is central to the walk of a son and daughter of God. Heaven wants you to know very quickly "this what my Father is" in this moment. This thing I am looking at, or holding, or considering, is not my Father. He is not this fear, this pain, this lack (or whatever). This kind of discernment is for the saints, and it flows from their alignment and focus on who He is, what He is, and how He is—all of that packaged together.

For instance, in Psalm 23 we read, "The Lord is My shepherd." The life-giving characteristics of a shepherd are also characteristics of your heavenly Father. You can engage those characteristics: His perfect love, His leading, His care to restore you, His feeding and watering of your life. Your heavenly Father is all these things and more to you.

Guardian angels are not designed to engage the enemy directly. Their chief purpose is as a protector, like a bodyguard, however they are not usually Warring Angels. Other angels are available to assist the Guardian Angel in the protection of someone's realm.

Angels provide help for humans in many ways and you can request angelic help for someone. At times, your angel or another persons' angel needs help, and you can request that from the Father. For instance, you detect a situation where an angel is having to contend with an enemy foray into a realm or gate. You can request of the Father Warring Angels to assist the persons angel and help bring about the defeat of the enemy.

As you learn about angels and realms, realize that you need to periodically check on the condition of all your realms. Since the revelation of realms is somewhat new, and it is understanding that is continuing to be expanded, the commissioning, charging, and loosing of your angel to guard your realm and its gates is an elementary teaching and understanding. You can also charge them to check on your realms, gates, and bridges to ensure that they are all secure. This can even be taught to children.

Learning to Possess Your Realm

It is a learning process to possess your realm. You are a realm and yet an individual is made up of many realms. The spirit of a person is a realm, their soul is a realm, their body is another realm. Their family constitutes a realm. A person's business or employment is a realm. Within these realms are territories.

Learning to possess your realm means learning what is in your realm that needs to go and learning what needs to come in. It is learning how it needs to be filled, how it needs to stay filled, and how angels help with that and work with that. It is also learning how to invite the characteristics and qualities of the Father into your realm. You want the fruit of the spirit in your realm. You experience that by yielding your realm and the territories of your realm to that working of the Holy Spirit.

You have different parts of your overall realm that are more associated with your humanity. For example, your soul is a realm within your overall realm. Your soul helps define your personality, your emotions, intellect, and more. When you think in terms of realms, you begin to ascertain their ability to change and all of this relies on your desire, your intention, and your choice.

The understanding of realms and how to possess them and give your angels charge to guard your realms are some of the things that the enemy has known for a long time and he used evil people to shut down. If he could not shut that understanding down in a person, he would steal it. He would steal their realm by filling it with himself.

Invite Jesus Into Your Realm

Those who are in the son, in Jesus, their first thing is to invite him into their realm. You have known this in a lens or perspective called salvation, and the effect is somewhat similar. You are inviting the living God in representation of Himself as His son Jesus to take up residence in your realm.

Deeding Your Territory

Inside every human realm exist territories. The soul realm has territories. Your physical flesh is a territory. Relationships are a territory, your speech is a territory, and you have many more.

One such territory is the territory of your imagination. An obstacle to our ability to see conclusively in the spirit realm is that the territory of our imagination has ownership claims against it by Satan, dark entities, or even people. Some of our territories have squatters residing on them. Those squatters need to go. We may have given access to these squatters by not policing the movies we watched, the songs we listened to, the magazines we read, or the television shows we gave time to.

Heaven has provided a simple solution to this issue. Simply transfer ownership of the territory of your imagination over to the Father, Son, and Holy Spirit. Let Him be the owner of that territory, and you become the steward. This can occur in the Court of Titles & Deeds, where we simply request that the Title Deed to the territory of our imagination be transferred to the Father, Son, and Holy Spirit. Also request that every squatter on that territory be evicted and removed.

Once this is completed, you will want to invite the King of Glory into the territory of your imagination. Welcome Him in, welcome Jesus and Holy Spirit, welcome the seven spirits of God, welcome the angelic hosts, welcome the men and women in white linen and welcome the living creatures of Heaven.

Guarding the Territory

Once the imagination is deeded to over to Him, the King helps you guard the territory of imagination in your realm, putting His assignment on it, putting His name on it, putting His label on it. Your imagination can be a well *and* a pool from which revelation is translated through now that the territory has His glory has His glory, His might, His power, and is a place of His dominion within your realm.

Filling Your Realm

Working with Holy Spirit to fill your realm with all of whom God is, and deeding these territories to Him for his use, is the true work of sons and daughters of God in their individual realm.

There are many voices that want entrance to your realm. You have been looking at the realm as a place and a deeded territory. You can also look at it from other dimensions. Look at it as sound frequency. What sound is in your realm and in the territories of your realm? What sound are you letting in? What visuals? What sensations? What are you allowing?

Compare and contrast your habits to the new thing God wants to give you. You cannot receive the new because you are involved in the habit. You must deed the habit to the Father, let him occupy that territory. Then you can tell the habit to get out of that realm and He will work with you in your realm to get that old habit out of your realm. You will say, "Oh, well, that habit has got to go. It has to get out of this realm." It may be necessary for you to repent for choosing or allowing that habit rulership in your life.

Once it exits that realm, then revelation can fill that space and create what you might call a new habit. You might call it a new functioning, or a new methodology of thought from which you live.

Your expression in your realm is precious to the Father, and yet the potential for its commodity of preciousness increases when you invite Him to fill your realm with more of Himself. In response, His glory fills more of it and your realm's value is increased. Your realm is enlarged.

Inviting Assignments into Your Realm

Then you have the whole thought of assignments. If we have lived from our soul, we often have inadvertently not allowed the plans and purposes of God to be released into our realms to begin their fulfillment. We simply did not know we needed to do so. Assignments are the purposes being pursued by, or within, a particular realm. Many facets need to be considered when contemplating assignments. Have you invited the assignments of God into your realm? Have you deeded the assignments in your realm to the King? Who owns the title deed of this assignment in itself? Is it the King? Or is it the enemy? Does the enemy have an assignment in this realm?

If you find that the enemy has an assignment in one of your realms, your job is to evict it. The way to do that is to deed the territory of the realm over to the King, so that the enemy no longer has any place. This action enables the angels of the King to provide back up to your realm, which further encourages the enemy to flee.

Many of the potential assignments are for the stewarding of the earth realm, or the earth as an entity. The earth is suffering because the assignments have not been taken up. Because we have not understood that our realms may have assignments, substitute assignments may have entered our lives. This can be reflected in career choices that are unfulfilling to a person. When you are doing what the Father planned for you to do while living on this planet, you find peace and contentment in what you are doing. When the proper assignments come into an individual's realm, and are deeded over to the King, then that individual begins to demonstrate all of what the Father has for them to steward the earth.

When Heaven says steward the earth, Heaven is talking about the physical earth which is about to begin to respond to the spiritual side of the children of God in amazing ways—ways we cannot even imagine.

You have already seen this in physical healings. If your body—your flesh body is made from the earth, then is not the earth also going to respond to the same in likewise manner? Absolutely. You have just not directed it to do so with the right language at the right moment. You need the glory of God to do that. You need His presence to do that.

Chapter 3

Understanding Angels

Many[6] have not understood the rankings of angels, the various assignments of angels and the various, what you would call, types of angels. We would call these races of angels, assignments of angels and levels of angels and is evident by their ranking. Most do not understand that angels rise through a ranking system that is an honor after which they seek.

One such type of angels is Appointed Angels. Appointed Angels have extremely large territories and responsibilities. Union, the angel over the United States of America is one such Appointed Angel. The Archangels are Appointed Angels: Michael, Gabriel, and Raphael. They have overarching duties over many in their realm.

Then there are Sent Angels carrying out instructions for every variety of Kingdom purpose. These angels are assigned to everything from working in heavenly courts, to ordering steps of people to fulfill the will of God, to

---

[6] This chapter is taken from a message by Donna Neeper.

carrying out scrolls, to bringing revelation, to rescuing humans physically. These are assigned and sent by the Heaven and many of them carry messages to people on the earth.

Many of us have understanding that we dialogue with the Father and Jesus, less so with the Holy Spirit, and even less with angels. This is changing, however. We are becoming aware of the fact that we do not need to be afraid when it comes to angels. This is a big break from much religious training that taught us to fear dialogue, interaction, and engagement with angels that Yahweh has created.

In coming days, the activity between angels and humanity will only increase as will the hunger of humans to begin to explore and understand working with angels. This is what we as a ministry are doing right now. We are giving room for exploration, discussion, and new thought regarding angels. Our YouTube audience hears this too because our reach goes further afield than we realize.

You could almost call this an awakening to the angelic realm for the bride of Christ. This is timely and in order. Heaven wants you to know, understand, and engage with angels and understand Holy Spirit may reveal your angel through your dreams. I encourage you to request of the Father a dream that reveals your angel(s) and any angels who are working with them.

Buckets of Thought

In our discussion of angels, we discovered we had various buckets of thought. Over time, we will likely find more buckets, but this is a good start for now. You will likely find yourself in one of these buckets.

Bucket #1
Beginning Engagement

You are learning to step into the realms of Heaven, see angels, as well as men and white women. You may be in this scenario.

Bucket #2
Dialoguing with Angels

If you are learning to work with your angel, calling your angel near, and dialoguing with your angel in the spirit. You are starting from the earth realm but seeing through the eyes of your spirit.

Bucket #3
Active Engagement

The third bucket is where you are actively engaging with angels and can see angels with your natural eyes.

Several people I have known were able to see angels with their natural eyes. We must understand that we have two sets of eyes – our spirit eyes and our natural eyes. When it comes to the supernatural realm, we often will see with our spirit eyes before we see with our natural physical eyes in the realm of the spirit.

Blake Healey who wrote *The Veil* is a unique individual who can see spiritual beings with his natural eyes when he chooses to look. Many of us can cultivate this ability. It likely will take practice, but I believe Heaven wants us to be able to do so.

In my book, *Unlocking Spiritual Seeing*, I identify typical blockages to spiritual sight that we have discovered in our years of working with people. If you are challenged in being able to see in the spirit realm, that book may be quite beneficial for you.

Chapter 4

Guardians & Their Realms

We need to talk about the realms, Ezekiel began. "An entangling of realms exists along with consequences born out of the entanglement of the realms within the saints. You may be suffering due to that entanglement and have need of a few things straightening out. You want to have access to the Guardian Angels of each realm involved and secure their employment to help straighten what has become tangled. With this we began our engagement with Heaven," he continued.

As a ministry, we are in a learning curve due to what we are doing. The ministry overall has achieved a higher level of responsibility. Unexpectedly, we found ourselves to be the target of a higher magnitude attack, whereby the demonic was, surprisingly, able to secure entry to our realm. It was like a raiding party against the ministry outreach, where the demonic is invading our realm with raiding parties for the purpose of making a mess, setting fires, causing general destruction, and loosing warfare weapons against our members and against the call of this ministry. Many things are changing along these lines. Your need for your angel's help is high and yet there is a door you must continue to approach and not back down. These were our instructions.

Your angel can use new weapons and more help. Some of what you are suffering from comes from the overall time in which you are living and the raiding parties of darkness against your calling and what has been granted to you. The enemy trembles and is fearful of what you can do and has picked out weaker members for plunder.

Heaven said this to us, "Your ministry contains realms and each person's realm associated with your ministry may provide to the enemy an open gate through which he attempts to deceptively enter. The need to transact courtroom business against him is urgent. You will find yourself in new courts for this and have need of greater understanding. Your work is causing discomfort to the enemy. By training new advocates, discovering new courtrooms and how to access them, and all the associated revelatory understandings that you are bringing to light, you are encroaching against the enemy. As a result, he wants to encroach upon you. He is trying to limit your territory because you are successfully taking back territory that he stole. His anger is stirred, but nevertheless, the Kingdom of God is victorious, and you must keep on this path and do not stop but continue to take steps as you know how and continue. Do not back down."

We sought more understanding of the entanglement of realms and about how to flow with and utilize the Guardian Angels of the realms. Ezekiel, the chief angel of our ministry began outlining his current needs: more arms, crossbows, javelins, smokescreen, nets, angel elixir, and maps to realms. He needed access to the map room. He needed an undergirding from his Commanding Angel and angel food and quietening for the quietening of atmospheres.

We made these requests of the Father on behalf of Ezekiel for his supply and the supply of his commanders and their ranks. Once we made the request, someone brought Ezekiel a key. It was the key to the map room.[7] He also asked for the weapon called stein,[8] so we made the request and off Ezekiel went.

Gates of the Realms

Each realm has gates that angels are supposed to guard. Guardians I am speaking of in this portion of the book are different from the Guardian Angels over the young. Your Personal Angel performs some of these duties but often you have other angels assigned to assist

---

[7] Maps indicate the lay of the land dimensionally for angels. It shows quicker pathways of travel for them and the location of gates, realms, bridges, traps, and trouble spots. When your angel asks for maps or for the key to the map room. Do not hesitate to request these things for them.

[8] Stein is a large stone that has directional capabilities. They come in various sizes. (Remember David's stone that slew Goliath).

in the guarding of every gate, realm, and bridge related to your life and ministry or business. The number of angels assigned is according to the scroll of the person or their business or ministry. They can be few or many according to the need and will of the Father. If ones' reach is limited the need for large amounts of angels is unnecessary. However, if the reach of your business or ministry is extensive, then you have need of more angels to guard the territories over which you have reach.

Since every person is a realm and has realms within their realm, those realms also have gates. The need of the person is for angels to guard the gates and realms as if on patrol or sentry duty. Also, because each person has bridges for the purpose of relationships and trade, those need to be guarded as well. Once you have engaged your angels and are cognizant of their assignment, charge them to patrol your realms, gates, and bridges only allowing that designated by the will of the Father and keeping out all that is not designed by the Father for you to experience or engage.

In the situation with LifeSpring, my Personal Angel and the chief angel over the ministry is Ezekiel. He has charge of other commanders who have charge of ranks of angels. These angels conduct sentry duty as well as work to bring those persons near to the ministry who are seeking the revelation and teaching we provide. They also work to keep hidden from our ministry those who are not assigned to know about us. Those not assigned to you can be a drain on your resources and time which is a type of theft. Theft of time or resources is not the desire of the Father for any of us and we need to be aware of that fact. In the past we have experienced working with those who were not assigned to work with us. It is a mutual assignment. As we trade with them, they are to trade with us. It is the way of Heavens' commerce.

The Guardian Angel of each realm should be on active duty, but often they are not. Some have been hijacked by the enemy. Some have been detained elsewhere. Some get stuck in other realms. Some like other realms, so they do not come back to the realm that they are assigned to. Some leave their post due to inactivity in their own realm or due to activity in other realms of which they are curious. They will leave their post and go to another realm because they recognize activity in that realm.

Angels like to be busy; they cannot stand to be bored. When angels see the activity in another realm, it may draw their curiosity and is a powerful attraction to Guardian Angels who are not being used by the owner of the realm to which they are assigned. The owner of the realm might be the son or daughter of God, or the human not yet awakened, or the darkened one[9] who has not received of the Father's renewal, rebirth, and salvation. As a result of the attraction of another realm, some angels have left their original assignment and have gone to view or participate in the activity in another realm. As

---

[9] Person who is not yet born again and awakened to the Kingdom of God.

they have done this without the permission of Heaven, they are essentially Absent With Out Leave (A.W.O.L.).

If you can determine that this is what has happened to a persons' angel, then to deal with this effectively requires courtroom work where the A.W.O.L. angel is taken to court for judgment. This takes place in the Court of Adjudication of Angelic Forces where you are not doing the judging, but the Father or those assigned by Him do the judging. As you bring the request to the court that a Guardian Angel has gone missing or has gone A.W.O.L., the court will weigh the evidence and decide the appropriate course of action. We will give a description of an experience we had in this court in the coming pages.

Angels who have left their post without permission are known as rogue Guardian Angels. Sometimes they leave their realm entirely for long periods of time, and do not return to where they have been posted. They are often curious about those who have active spiritual realms and may not want to participate in realms of darkness from darkened humanity. They sometimes even desire escape routes from their realm, lest they be put to the task of engaging darkness, because this is not their purpose against their design. They may be resisting their assignment and often are taken captive by darkness to be forced by unenlightened humanity[10] or the

---

[10] Witches and warlocks often utilize these rogue Guardian Angels for their purposes.

demonic realm to do the deeds of darkness. This is a very tragic and disconcerting thing to the angels of Heaven. I discuss the aspect of angels in captivity in Chapter 7.

It is important that humanity awaken to their God-given role as stewards of the realms – important for humans and for angels. Without proper stewardship of the realms, both humans and angels risk capture by the enemy, instead of co-laboring together to bring about the purposes of God for their realm.

It is not uncommon for angels to petition the Father for reassignment from the human realms that they have been charged with stewarding. Do you see how our misunderstanding of angels has impacted our lives and the lives of so many?

Do you know when a person receives the light of the Father through Jesus, the Son, and begins the journey of grace to become sons and saints, there is much rejoicing in Heaven because the angel of that realm has been upgraded too? It is like a redemption. It is not like the angel is redeemed, but *the angel receives the redemption of their realm when the human is redeemed.* The angels have even greater pleasure when a person receives Jesus than when a saint returns home to Heaven (passes away).

The realms of humanity have not understood the spiritual realm that they are the steward over. They have not known this. They have not seen this. Many saints are still darkened in their understanding—not understanding their role to adjudicate angels, to command angels, to stir angels, to rescue angels, and to pursue angelic activity with demand and certainty. This is changing, but this understanding is a great need of mankind.

Some who work from darkness who have this understanding, and they have released pillaging, illegal trade, gross human conflict, and the outworking of captured thrones through their understanding of the angelic realm. This is grievous.

It is important that the saints better understand the angelic race, so that realms can be stewarded and traded from as the Father designed. The Bride must continue in her maturity, taking up all things the Father has released and given to her through the Son, for is she not the Bride of the greatest one?

This release of power coming to the Bride is not because she lacks power. It is because she has failed to steward her realms; and they have subsequently been lost through her lack of understanding. Heaven desires humanity to open their eyes and see what darkness has done and how the Bride has been stolen from in this regard.

It is time for the Bride to take this back. It is part of her narrative. It is part of who she is. It is part of her manner of being. The bride has not understood this and has not been able to work together as a body in this area—but this is changing. Heaven always has hope, and Heaven releases this hope to you.

Overthrowing Thrones

The demonic thrones upon the earth must be overthrown. Who is going to do that? It is the angelic forces of Heaven managed by the members of the Bride—those who are awakened and have authority, knowing who they are, knowing their assignment, and their calling. This will stop the earth from being plundered and raped and will bring to a halt the illegal trade that is going on between the many dimensions and realms.

The Next Great Awakening

Some humans offer their allegiance to illegal wicked thrones. The Bride needs to awaken and remove these illegal usurpers by establishing the angelic who are rightfully assigned to these thrones. Until the Bride does, most of these angelic assignees are captured and kept in chains in the spiritual realms. This is a part of the next great awakening—the awakening of humanity to who they really are. This is one of the things that causes Satan to tremble as humanity awakens to their spiritual self and the power of the Father is released through the Son to them, both corporately and individually; but even more that the personal awakening, but also the awakening to their ability to work with angels.

The shaking of thrones in Heaven and in heavenly places right now is quite thrilling. It is at such a height of activity right now.

I want you to understand that Heaven sees the timeline of earth. Heaven understands the times and seasons and participates from their position in the Father's Kingdom with a great many understandings that cannot be released to earth yet.

Satan has long had a ploy against humanity to force them (almost as if to give them a false commandment) to only know the physical realm.

Heaven told us that Adam understood all realms, as well as the realm that he was going to steward (the 3-D plane or the earth realm). The awakening of humanity to their spirituality from the goodness, light, kindness, power, might, glory dimension of Yahweh revealed to the sons of God is what will begin to shift and change in the next era, along with the recognition these things by the many saints who have long been blinded to these understandings.

Removing the Veil

Blindness is not when you walk around with your eyes shut. Blindness is where you walk around with something over your eyes. It is the tearing of the veil off the eyes that is so needed in this era. It is so urgently mandated from Heaven, that even angel forces have been loosed to this regard, but they are still in great warfare in the heavens while their assignment has not yet been fully equated into their victory.

Adjudication of Angelic Forces

Heaven explained, "Some of your angels have left their post and gone to other realms." Other angels having left their post have been captured by darkness and need to be freed. Whenever a Guardian Angel is not at their post, the realm(s) they have been assigned to have not been stewarded and are vulnerable to intrusion.

For those who have left their post, you need to appear in the Court of Adjudication of Angelic Forces. This is not where angels dwell to receive assignments, nor is this is the court where angels can meet with you. This is the court where they are judged. "Heaven is ready for you to bring a case in that court on behalf of the two angels assigned to your ministry who have left their post. They have gone A.W.O.L.," we were told.

We asked Lydia to accompany us to this court and were led to the Court of Adjudication of Angelic Forces.

Lydia acted as our counselor. She began, "We bring forth a case regarding two Guardian Angels who have left their post. We bring it to this Court of Adjudication of Angelic Forces. We enter in the request for this court that two angels of realms connected to LifeSpring International Ministries have gone A.W.O.L. We request of this court a verdict ruling to receive them back to their post."

In the court they began looking into these angel's assignments and were verifying that we had a case regarding these two A.W.O.L. angels.

Lydia explained more how this court worked. She said this court first verifies your charge against the angel. Then, the court releases their agreement where these angels have left their post. Remember, these are Guardian Angels who have left their posts.[11] The court will decide.

Others were in the courtroom. We saw magistrates of the realms who seemed to have great interest in our case. The magistrates were helping to bring a ruling in the case. They also act as the angel's representatives. They are like the angel commanders and they take up the case from here. They would not initiate such a process unless a human brought a case.

She explained, "If you did not bring the case, it could not move forward, However, since we brought the case, the ruling came from the court, who with the angel

---

[11] Sometimes referred to as rogue Guardian Angels.

magistrates and the angel commanders' representatives, deliberated the case back and forth.

Continuing to watch, we could see the Just Judge who was releasing his judgment regarding these A.W.O.L. angels. The Just Judge ruled on behalf of us and released the verdict. He released a Judgment of these angels for dereliction of duty. He ordered that they be reprimanded and reassigned back to their post—only this time, they would come under an order where they are required to check in or be noticed by someone (like a parole officer).

We asked, "When do we know it's effect?"

"Simply trust that it will have an effect," we were told.

Lydia went on to explain that we could request this court to release the Father's goodness to these angels. This is almost like where we stand in the place of requesting mercy for them; otherwise, they are judged severely from the Just Judge. Our request that the Father release mercy to these angels was also heard in this court. We were told we could stand and ask the Just Judge that he be merciful as this is a first-time offense for these angels.

We announced to the court, "We are in agreement with the release of the Father's goodness to these angels."

Following the court proceedings, we went to a conference room. Lydia began to explain, "Now that the Guardian Angels have been dealt with in the court, they will be re-installed at the gate of the realms. It is now your job to command them to secure the gate of the realm that they have been assigned, to patrol it with veracity and strength, and to maintain it against every intruder. These Guardian Angels will be at a heightened awareness of your speaking to them."

We asked about the other realms associated with the ministry.

One or two other realms were not secured, meaning the angel of that realm had not been stirred to their duty which occurs by commissioning your angel to your realm. Angels know their assignment to a realm as it is in a scroll that they possess. However, part of our co-laboring with them is to verbally commission them to the fulfillment of their duties over their realm. Lydia explained, "It is not that these angels are not strengthened. They are busy, but not as busy as they should have been, not having been as stirred to their duty."

We inquired, "It sounds like we can release a stirring to each angel connected to the ministry, so that they are awakened to their duty to guard the gate of their assigned realm?"

"Yes, this can be done by proclamation where you join forces with Ezekiel to release an announcement that you are watching and taking note of the realms connected to your realm and your trading floor," Lydia explained.

We asked, "Do you request the stirring up of each Guardian Angel at the gate of their realm, so that they increase their duty and are empowered to their mandate?"

Lydia replied, "Yes. This accomplishes a stirring in the atmospheres of the realms and is almost as if it is the completion of a cycle that was once broken. You achieve this by a verbal commission of the angel to fulfill their duty to the realm to which they have been assigned."

She continued, "Now, you understand the gates of the realms that are connected to the realm[12] and trading floor of the ministry. Simply speak to these angels to accomplish their duty. The angels will know when you speak it.

You can release Ezekiel to check on them. He has enough ranks. He will command his ranks as you ask him to check on the guardians of the gates of the realms associated to your realm.

Ezekiel can help you understand where there are other guardians of their gates who are in danger, or who need something, or who get captured, or are A.W.O.L. He can help you understand that too.

Be sure to request Ezekiel's assistance in this. He can check in on them. You also need to ask Ezekiel to strengthen the two that have been re-established to their

---

[12] Some realms have within them other realms. Those inner realms may also have realms within.

post. It is almost like they need a buddy angel for a while."

. . . .

We were then instructed by Lydia to welcome the two angels back to their post and commission them according to their mandate.

We did as Lydia directed, and had the sense that something was plumped up. It looked like fireworks—when you see one burst in the air and then the embers come floating back down to earth.

As you inquire of Heaven concerning your angels, you may find a similar scenario. For those of you who have a business or ministry, you will need to check on the status of the angels related to those entities.

In the next two chapters we discuss working with your angels. You will find some helpful information as you learn how to sense their presence and how to engage with them.

Chapter 5

How to Work with Your Angel

Part 1

It works like radar. Just as a submarine would detect an object on a radar screen, it works similarly with angels. Thus Ezekiel, our ministry's angel, began his instruction to us.

"Does the angel have me on radar, or do I have an angel on radar?" Donna inquired.

Ezekiel replied that it works both ways. Your angel always knows where you are, as if the angel can see you on radar. Wherever that angel is, whatever the angel is doing, the angel is aware of where you are and what you are doing via the angel's radar. It is not quite like a submarine radar screen, but that gives you an idea of how it works. Ezekiel was helping us recognize that this is the method used by angels. They have that ability.

"So, you are saying we can learn to use this same sonar pathway or frequency of wave link communication to tune into where you are?" we asked.

"That is what you have to use," was his reply. Whenever you need angelic help, the presence of Heaven, or the near presence of the Father, the Son or the Holy Spirit, an angel can bring that to you.

Angels bring various things. To you, it feels like the presence of the Holy Spirit, but that is really a result of your inability to discern the different levels of the presence of angles or Holy Spirit. As a child of God who is maturing and beginning to discern different anointings or different expressions of the presence, angels are involved in this.

You can grow in your understanding and your discerning of spirits and what the angels bring. You can discern angels that bring a healing anointing, angels that bring a fire anointing, angels that bring revelation, and anointing angels. While you may not perceive the angel itself, you are perceiving the anointing. You are perceiving what they bring or what they carry. What you are really perceiving is their frequency waves.

A Healing Angel has a different frequency than a revelation angel or a fire angel and you are perceiving them by frequency. Often people are trying to look for them—but they need to discern them first via frequency. It is easier to do it that way. The auditory and visual frequencies are different.

"I discern them, and after my discernment, then I can look. Usually, as I look in the spirit realm, I begin to get the details of what the angel was like," Donna described to me.

You have a radar function in your spirit that discerns the presence of angels. Most believers have this ability yet have never activated it because they do not know how to use it. These believers are like infants who have been given the keys to the car, but only put them in their mouth. Knowing how to use this radar function is a marker of the growth of one's spirit through the understanding of the spirit realm in Jesus Christ; combined with the boldness to enter that realm by leaving fear behind.

"You are going to get it wrong on occasion, but that is part of the learning and growing process," Ezekiel said with a smile.

What You Seek, You Find

When you seek for the Father with all your heart, you are going to find the Father. You are going to find His realm. You are going to get what you seek for. If you are seeking for darkness, you are going to get darkness. If you are seeking for light, you are going to get light.

"Do you see the employment of your faith here?" Ezekiel asked. "You face forward from your spirit. You are looking for the Kingdom of Light. The access point is always Jesus. Therefore, the access point is usually praise and as you praise, your spirit comes forward, your soul recedes, and you can employ your spiritual discernment better," he continued.

Some do have the ability to see, seemingly with their natural sight—their natural eyeball. They use their natural eyeball to see angels or to see in the spirit realm, but they are seeing with both sights, spiritual and natural. Your spiritual sight is connected on some level to your natural sight. However, when a person is dying, they may sense spiritual realities more readily, because other senses are already shutting down. As other senses are shutting down prior to death, one's spiritual sight often increases.

You discern through your sensor—your knower. You have discerned numerous angels—individual angels as well as groups of angels at times. They may not have looked like the pictures in Guidepost or Angels magazines, but you have seen them.

When an angel wants to be made known, it *will* be made known. Some angels are present with you at times, but they are intentionally hiding themselves from your discerner or your knower for a variety of reasons. Some angels need you to acknowledge their presence, however. They are present and they need your understanding and your engagement with them.

"Is that like co-laboring?" Donna asked.

Ezekiel replied in the affirmative and went on to explain that it is a form of co-laboring. As Ezekiel was speaking, he reminded Donna of an example of this that occurred a few days before when she was on a Zoom call with several friends. As she was praying and releasing Godly bonds into a situation and severing ungodly bonds, a huge angel presented himself to Donna. That angel needed her to discern its presence, so that this prayer group could release the angel to do its work—which is exactly what they did.

In fact, when that angel stepped in, Donna asked the angel, "What do I need to do?" He instructed her to release him to do his work, and she knew when the angel left.

The Power of Desire

"Can everybody operate in that?" we wanted to know.

Everyone can to some degree, based on their desire. Sometimes this is called their hunger to do so, based on their curiosity and awakening to the realms of the spirit. Sooner or later, they are going to hunger and thirst after the activity of operating with angels because this is the Father's design—that the realm of the spirit and angels would work with the realm of the earth and children of God. There are many more angels at work in the earth realm than are being perceived or discerned.

"Is there some way we can help jumpstart this awakening with people?" we asked.

Ezekiel replied, "Teach people that their angels hearken to them more than they are aware." Angels are often assigned to assist the growing awakening of the saint. Your angel has likely been at work helping you become awakened to his or her presence. If you asked to be awakened to their presence, it was your angel who facilitated your desire to ask to be awakened.

Finding the Fear

To help people cooperate with their angel(s), begin by having them comb through their understanding of angels and begin to form questions about what they are afraid of. Fear, in any dimension—whether in thought, heart belief, experiences as a youth, or dimensional presences that you did not know the source of—can result in fear being embraced, even if unintentional.

Where do you have a personal fear of seeing angels? It may be very subtle. You may have been tricked by the enemy to think that you might see a demon instead! Be assured, if you have asked the Father to see your angel, He will be glad to respond and facilitate that for you.

Once you have identified any fear associated with seeing angels or seeing in the realm of the Spirit, submit the fear to the Father for cleansing and purification. Then request a fresh flow from the Father—a new mindset, and an angel to come to teach you and awaken you.

These angels will awaken and teach any who seek and desire, but often it is the presence of fear on any level that hinders the awareness of angels.

Fear may appear like a dimensional thing—not necessarily a demon or a principality, but like a belief that something that seems insurmountable. Demons will often put you into a moment of trauma or a moment of a scare. They will use a scare tactic to get your soul to align with fear in agreement that you never want to do that again. That is one of the bigger blocks and it is in your soul. Perhaps it was a horror movie that brought about the occasion where fear came in. Repent for exposing yourself to that movie and ask the Father's forgiveness. Then ask Him to restore anything that was stolen from you, because of your surrender to fear.

The more you step into your spirit and the more you live from your spirit, the more natural it becomes to converse and engage with angels. This cannot be accomplished from your soul—conversing with angels, sensing their presence, and harmonizing with their frequency. Your soul does not have the capacity to understand the frequency of the angels. You must be living from your spirit to understand and to be in that dimensional, spiritual frequency to resonate with your angel. Therefore, the scripture says to worship in spirit and truth. The frequency to engage with your angel operates via truth, not deception, and operates within the spirit arena, not the soul's arena.

Worship Opens Portals

Worship opens portals where angels come frequently. They love to be around worship because they cannot wait to worship. The frequency for this is called focus—it is where a saint focuses to worship Jesus, or to worship the Father. The soul holds the desire, and the natural thought comes to begin to worship, but as you do, you are meant to press through to your spirit and allow your spirit to come forth. That switch is like morphing. Then, when you are *in spirit* and you worship, your discernment is heightened and that is when you will know the presence of angels. Since angels operate on frequency, when the right one (such as in my wife Adina's music[13]) is being released, and your spirit agrees with that frequency, your discernment or awareness harmonizes with the angels that have come.

Donna had another question for Ezekiel. "When you have no fear, but you recognize a need to speak to your angel, can you describe how that works and what it's like when you do it wrong and when you do it right?"

When you do it wrong, you act like a toddler throwing a tantrum when they want a toy that their parent has put away. You want something immediately. For instance, you see something that is unjust, or you have a moment of panic, and in that moment, you are operating from

---

[13] Adina Horner's music is available at www.adinasmelodies.com.

your soul and scream out for what you need. Acting out of that soul frequency does not help you at all. It does not achieve anything, but sometimes people act from that side of themselves. That is where you need to quiet your soul, press into your spirit, and call your spirit forward.

Moving from Soul to Spirit

From their spirit, a spirit-filled believer first harmonizes with Holy Spirit to know what to do. It is the practice of moving from soul to spirit that quickens your spirit person with faster, more frequent, and easier co-laboring conversations, as well as more regular engagement with angels. Moving from the spirit is always better than moving from the soul. This is the mark of maturity for a child of God becoming a son of God.

"Recognition of the goodness of the Father, gratefulness, thankfulness, intent, and desire help you step over into your spirit," Ezekiel explained. "It is related to frequency. It is harder to step into your spirit when the frequency in your atmosphere is saturated with the natural realm."

Donna explained that Ezekiel was giving an example of when she speaks to someone who is talking from their logical brain and is analyzing facts. Donna would rather pursue the answer from the spirit but sometimes feels blocked. The reason for the blockage is because her friend had made an agreement to be in the soul only.

Doing so affects the frequency of the atmosphere, which causes a person who wants to be spiritual, who wants to step into their spirit or wants to operate from their spirit, to struggle with doing so. It is more difficult, though not impossible. He went on to explain that often, you must come away from that environment and change the atmosphere where you are. Donna likes to turn on Adina's music, and she has a diffuser because she sometimes needs to change the smell of the atmosphere. That is what going to a "secret place" in your closet is all about.

Many intercessors are getting exceptionally good at this and appreciate the secret place closet and the ease for prayer and worship they find in that place because it is akin to a portal or pathway to Heaven.

Chapter 6
How to Work with Your Angel
Part 2

As we continued learning how to work with your angel, more understandings were given to better enable and strengthen that engagement.

The Power of Agreement

Working in the spirit realm pertains to one's level of agreement to allow their spirit to engage with Holy Spirit. If fear is present, one cannot work in the spirit realm effectively because the fear will limit you. Your agreement comes from your spirit, which must speak to your soul and say, "No, we are going to do this." The soul will step down and, with practice, you will be able to press through the veil. When you are operating from your spirit, you harmonize frequencies with your angel. Your angel knows immediately when you are doing that.

Each person must learn what their trigger for engaging with Heaven and the realm of the spirit is. It seems to be somewhat unique to the person. That is the point of seeking; to seek what works for you is a sign of hunger and maturing as a saint.

Always seek what works for you.

When people are together with you, set the atmosphere by opening a portal through a sound frequency[14] and by inviting angels, you have made it easy for people to experience Heaven. Setting the atmosphere by finding the frequency of Heaven and inviting the angels to come near will create an ease of accessing Heaven.

Test out what works best for you to engage with Heaven and the realm of the spirit.

The Stance and the Sound

For some, what works to engage with Heaven and the realm of the spirit is a specific physical and spiritual stance. For others, the physical stance of stepping into the realms of Heaven blocks them. With some people, it is the sound. For still others, it is the knowledge of what it would be like to be taught by angels—the knowledge that they are soul and spirit and *they are able to be what*

---

[14] Anointed worship/soaking music.

and how the Father created them, with the ability to be spiritual.

Many are held captive by religious training that has shut the door to their spirit side, mainly due to fear. Much fear has been taught from pulpits. The enemy has had a heyday with this because anyone who has learned to fear will be fearful—and when you seek fear, that is what you get.

Anyone who has been taught fear will be fearful.

Do not Cooperate with Fear

One of my instructions related to Heaven down is to teach people not to seek fear. You must understand that **you cannot agree with fear and seek the Kingdom of Light at the same time.** It will *not* work. Your soul will overrule your spirit because of that belief system.

When teaching people how to step into Heaven, I tell them that junk (the demonic) is not invited to the party. Because it is not invited, I have never had to deal with any. The reason is that I have my focus pointed toward Heaven, not toward the supernatural arena in general. For you, it will be determined by where your focus is pointed. Let me remind you to do an internal check—where are you directing your focus?

People often do not realize where their focus is. They do not realize they have the innate ability from the Father to choose to point their focus toward fear or faith, to darkness or light. Most people have not been taught about focusing intentionally.

Bloodline Beliefs

Ezekiel continued to explain that another thing at work which must be dealt with is bloodline beliefs. He gave a few examples to help us understand.

Mockery

One thing that shuts down the ability to engage with angels in a bloodline is mockery. This can manifest as mockery of the Holy Spirit, mockery of the Kingdom, mockery of the realms of the spirit, mockery of the blessings of God, or mockery of the names of God—in short, mockery in nearly any form creates a blockage or a hindrance. Some may not know that this exists as an iniquity of their bloodline. Mockery that is multigenerational is certainly an iniquitous pattern in many families. If you recognize it in your family, you must repent for it.

How do I know if it is in my life? Ask yourself, "Have I ever mocked Benny Hinn, Oral Roberts, or Kathryn Kuhlman? Have I mocked the late D. James Kennedy, Billy Graham, Franklin Graham, or other evangelists or ministers? Is mockery of the supernatural a habitual issue in my family line? If I see a healing take place, do I mock it or doubt its validity? If the answer to any of these questions is yes, you have an iniquity in your bloodline—mockery. Any time I mock, I am placing myself in a position of judgement over the validity of something. Since you and I may do a poor job of judging correctly, we should leave that to the Father—the Just Judge.

The Church, since its infancy, has mocked the spiritual side of things. The adversary has promoted the idea that spiritual matters are fairy tales, weird, or simply nonsensical—and has encouraged this mockery.

You must repent for agreeing with the spirit of mockery and for any mockery in your own life, whether wittingly or unwittingly. You must also repent for carrying around the attitude that "I am going to look at this, but I might mock it," which is a form of judgment, or "I am going to reserve the right to mock this." The Church, in its early days, did that quite a lot. Therefore, it is in a lot of bloodlines.

Most of you reading this book are likely in the "charismatic" camp. Perhaps, prior to your embrace of this form of belief, you may have mocked those "holy rollers," or "tongue talkers," or "mystics." If so, repentance may be in order.

Like any generational bloodline cleansing, we seek the blood of Jesus to cleanse the bloodline by purification of the mocking. We must deal with this because a spirit of mocking exists that seeks to corrupt bloodlines and hinder them from experiencing the supernatural arena. We need to repent of the mocking and forgive, bless, and release those who introduced it into the family line, and do the same for all who perpetuated it throughout the generations. We must also repent of our own mockery. After doing this, we ask for a cleansing of all the impact and ramifications of the mockery, and release blessing to those who were mocked. Request the restoration of your ability to cooperate with Heaven which has been affected by the mockery in your bloodline.

Fear

Fear, which we have already discussed, can also be a generational iniquity. If you recognize it, repent, and ask the blood of Jesus to cleanse you and your bloodline. You must deal with fear in the bloodline as well as mockery. Just as generational mocking requires repentance, you also need to request to be made sensitive so that you do not agree with mocking or fear in the future.

Shutting Down Spiritual Sensitivity

Many parents need to repent where they have shut down the spiritual knowings (or sensitivity) of small children. Often, this is demonstrated in the imaginative growth of their child or where the child has had a dalliance with imagination that is linked to the Holy Spirit (and not an evil or demonic spirit). Small children are very spiritual. They are incredibly open, like a little open gate. They often have no preconceived fear. Most fears are instilled by the parent. Parents' descriptions of the "boogey man" and similar things often instilled unnecessary fear in their children. Parents often put a boundary line on their child's imagination and on the spirit realm as it pertains to their child. That must be repented for in the bloodline as well because it is possible your parents did this to you. They may have taught you to be afraid of angels and other appearances.

This is not to say that a parent would intentionally shut this down in a child. More often, it is because the parent does not have a grid for the operations of the spirit in their own life, much less in the life of their child. Or the parent does not want to deal with it because *they* have a fear of it, so they shut it down in the child without even knowing it at times.

Some shut down the use of the imagination for cultural reasons. They want their child to be "normal". A child with an active imagination and who talks with angels may be considered odd and abnormal. It is the parent's fear of man that makes them shut the child's imagination down. Generations have been captured by false boundary lines due to parents doing this.

The antidote to that is the parents learning to trust in God. The parents must learn to trust in the goodness of the Father. A parent's trust and subsequent disagreement with the belief that this is something to be feared is vital. When humanity begins to understand that this sensitivity of children to spiritual things is a pathway to the Father from a very young age, it will change our understanding of everything from evangelism, to salvation, to operating from spirit first and soul second.

---

*Imagine a generation
with no fear in their spirit.*

This is possible in our era. This is what our enemy is most afraid of and wants to close off.

Activating the Pure Flow of the Spirit

The pure flow of the spirit that one is born with must be activated. Some people teach that when you are born, your spirit is not awake, but your spirit **is** awake and has been since the moment of conception. It is just not activated, practiced, utilized, or addressed.

Learn to step into Heaven on a regular basis. People *need* to step into Heaven. It is a good practice and people need to be reminded how busy Heaven is. They need to be reminded that the activity level that Heaven operates from is instantaneous. Heaven always wants to relate to them and to communicate, talk, and assist them in the 3-D realm.

Many more spiritual beings than we know want to be engaged. Heaven has unlimited availability and desires to communicate with you, so build an expectation for when you step into heavenly realms. Expect to receive *from* Heaven and expect to communicate *with* Heaven.

You need to experience the flowers, the trees, and the sentient beings in Heaven. Once you have stepped into Heaven, you have stepped through the veil. This is the reason Jesus opened the veil of the Temple—to create clear access to the presence of God. The veil of the Temple blocked access to the Ark of the Covenant to all but a few individuals throughout history. Once Jesus surrendered his spirit, the veil of the Temple was rent from top to bottom.[15]

Therefore, religion was never going to cut it. Heaven has always been about relationship and reality—and that is a dimensional word.

Limitless Expectation

"Do you remember when you recognized one day that you saw a limit in your life where you thought you could only call out to the Father, and you wondered why you had not been calling out to Jesus too? Then, after a period, you came into an understanding of Holy Spirit and you then wondered why you had never called out to Holy Spirit. It dawned on you that you had not communicated with the Godhead—the Trinity," Ezekiel inquired of Donna.

---

[15] Matthew 27:51, Mark 15:38, Luke 23:45

He answered his own question by saying, "It is because you were taught the expectation that it was limited to you, that the Father was not interested even in speaking to you, but only that you would speak to Him. That comes from mindsets that people learned early on. Re-teaching is necessary, the practice of accessing Heaven is necessary, and the engagement of angels is necessary. Fear is simply the big stumbling block."

Activating Your Spirit Eyes

Many people are trying to engage with their angel using their natural eyeball rather than concentrating on their spiritual sight.

Often, people are trying to see something like a movie with their natural eyes in the 3-D realm. It is not that seeing spiritually is that different, but it *is* a different set of eyes that are used to see in the spirit realm. It is your spirits eyes, rather than your body's eyes.

When it comes to seeing in the spirit, sometimes you see only an outline, especially when you are just beginning, and you simply do not see much. However, you must keep looking.

The more you look,
the more you will see!

The more you focus, and the more you slow down with the intent to see, the more details you will see.

Seeing and hearing work in tandem. That is another thing people do not understand.

> *Some need to know that*
> *their hearing can trigger their seeing*
> *and some need to understand*
> *their seeing can trigger their hearing.*

Why would you just use one sense when you are meant to use them all? You can even blow people's minds by saying, "Use your sense of spiritual smell. It is a sense. It all works together. Just like with your physical body, your natural senses all work together. Most people's natural senses work together more than they know to interpret the natural realm. It is the same thing—only you are using all your spiritual senses to interpret the realm of the spirit.

We have discussed your sight and hearing, but have you ever felt heat in your hands when you laid hands on someone? If so, that was a manifestation of Heaven through physical touch.

Have you ever smelled a wonderful fragrance that had no natural source? You were experiencing Heaven manifesting through smell.

Yes, you can even taste to discern. For example, have you ever shared Communion and the wine or juice you were consuming seemed quite different from what you knew it to be naturally? That may have been Heaven infusing your time of Communion with a supernatural event.

Ezekiel, the Old Testament prophet, had multi-sensory visionary encounters. He could see, hear, touch, and smell the elements in the visions he experienced. You can experience the same type of thing! Expect it!

This is a very uncommon area of discussion. There is teaching and there is discussion—two different things. Teaching is good, but then you need to have discussion. You must have time for questions. You also must have time for processing the information. That is where you are. All this seems to come from where you are focused.

Donna was reminded of a time when she was taught about spiritual smell and she went through a period where she was focused on what she was smelling in the spirit. Because she was focused on the sense of smell, she could smell more.

When you pick up a pair of binoculars, you do so with the intent of focusing on something far away you cannot see well without assistance. Put on your spiritual binoculars to look and focus.

Have you ever looked through binoculars and found they are not focused on what you are looking for or you have not found it in the sight? Everything is blurry and you are not sure where or how far away the object is. You must focus for a minute to find the object you are looking for. This is remarkably like what we are suggesting for achieving spiritual focus.

Donna and I follow the same procedure when accessing the Business Complex. When we step into the heavenly realms, we look for the Help Desk. We can see the things we are looking for because we are focused on finding them.

Donna went on to describe how she grew in this ability, "I stepped in with seeking and I allowed it to be presented." As she allowed it to be presented, it was.

"When you step in and you want to meet with me, what do you do?" Ezekiel asked.

"I step in, I ask for you. I wait, then I focus to look. I look around. I may ask, 'Where are you?' until I see you. Today I saw you come around the corner into the lobby area because I was looking for you," Donna commented.

"That is desire. That is seeking. That is waiting," Ezekiel replied.

"Remember when the Father told you about the Cotton Candy Dream?" Ezekiel asked Donna.

"Yes," she replied, and then she began to unfold the story of the Cotton Candy Dream that she uses to teach people how to step into spiritual realms. One of the nuances of the dream was about to how be a child. You need to be a child in the presence of complete acceptance, goodness, and unconditional love—where everything was good and nothing negative existed. That is how small children believe. That is what little kids come into the earth realm with. However, over time they lose that ability.

One day the Lord said to Donna, "I want to talk to you about the cotton candy dream." Donna did not know what he was talking about, so over the course of four or five days, he gave her an understanding of what blocks vision in the heavenly realm. In the natural realm we often experience an inability to engage childlikeness easily.

He said, "Think of the product you call cotton candy. Cotton candy is something that you get only at certain places, but every time you get it, or every time a child gets it, it is in a fun atmosphere. You get it at a park, festival, fair, carnival, or a ballpark. There is nothing good nutritionally in cotton candy. There is not one speck of vitamins or minerals, only calories and a lot of food coloring. Imagine that a small child sees this pink cotton candy and says, 'Oh, I want that.' It looks so good. It looks as if it would feel wonderful. It is unusual. There is excitement because it is special, but the parent always says no."

He continued, "Then, one day the parent says 'yes', and the child cannot believe they finally have access to this cotton candy."

The Father asked, "Why would the parents say yes?"

Donna explained, "I don't know, why would the parent say yes because there is no inherent good in cotton candy?"

He said, "Just because it was the hope and dream of the child."

It is the dream that adults miss. That is what shuts down creativity and vision for the future in the natural realm.

Imagine that you are the child who wants the cotton candy, and your parent says yes. You can have as much cotton candy as you want. On top of that, imagine that this cotton candy has no negatives attached to it. It is just cotton candy and you get to have as much as you want. That could unlock something in an adult because they have lost the ability to think like that. The expectation of receiving goodness been shut down.

You judge your answer before you have even dreamed your dream.

Donna shared this story with a lady who was a breast cancer survivor. She is James Nesbit's (the prophetic artist) wife, Coleen. Apparently, sharing the Cotton Candy Dream really touched her, because the next day James sent Donna a graphic[16] and he said, "You need to use this graphic when you talk about that because it was meaningful to Coleen. She did not realize she had shut down seeing in her life."

The Father instructed Donna to use that dream to help people understand how to step into the spirit realm. This brings the freedom to *just be childlike* and not worry about anything, but this wonderful ability to have cotton candy with no negatives.

This story could be a key to helping people realize their self-given limits or self-given parameters, where they see the defenses they erected and said, "I will never cross that." Many people have put up fences they do not even realize exist until they hear a story like "The Cotton Candy Dream," and they realize they have limited themselves. This could help them see these fences and knock them down. If you realize you have a fence, do a prophetic act of pushing down that fence and walking into that next place.

Ezekiel explained that a hunger exists for this. People do want to break down their own barriers. Part of that is because it is a function of the realization that, "It is time

---

[16] More beautiful artwork available at www.jamesnesbit.com

for this. It is time for the Bride to walk into this. It is time for her to become known for this. It is time for her to be brave about this and it is time for the walls of religion to fall."

Helping Your Angel

Just because you have an angel does not mean that your angel always has all he needs to work on your behalf. Angels have needs, and you can learn to be sensitive to those needs, to help keep him or her functioning at maximum capacity.

How to Arm Them Up

On a very regular basis, we will ask our angel to come near and ask him if he needs anything. Sometimes he lets us know he is fine, while at other times he will have specific requests for us. When angels have needs arising from their service to us, we must make the requests of the Father on their behalf. They cannot do it themselves. Angels are not sons and daughters of the Most High, so they do not have the same standing that we do. This ensures a co-laboring between humans and the angelic realm.

For instance, Ezekiel has, on occasion, requested more arrows, so we petition the Father for arrows for Ezekiel, the ministry angel for LifeSpring International Ministries, and his ranks. (He has charge over other angels who assist him). It is as simple as that. Some of the things we have been asked to request are as follows:

- Arrows
- Bow & Arrows
- Swift Bows
- Crossbow
- Fiery Arrows
- Fiery Darts
- Fiery Rocks
- Fireballs
- Fire Pebbles—goes into crevasses where darkness is hiding and lights it up
- Explosives in a pouch
- Slingshots (aka Goliath Killers)
- Axes
- Sledgehammers
- Spears
- Short swords
- Scintars—small swords
- Scimitars—large, curved swords
- Swords
- Broadswords
- Shields
- Ropes
- Lassoes
- Binding Instruments
- Chains
- Smoke

- Smoke Screen—provides concealment in a battle situation
- Flail—spiked ball connected by a chain to a wooden handle. Used to go around the shield of an enemy combatant.
- Weapons for hand-to-hand combat
- New armor
- Hourglass
- Timed Devices
- Encircling—an incendiary object
- Backup—sometimes they need more angels to assist them in their work, particularly when in battle
- More firepower—at times more weaponry is needed, but not necessarily more angels.
- Frequency bombs
- Dragnets
- Nets—useful for the capture of exceedingly small entities
- Bird Nets
- Chaos Nets—arrests chaos over an area
- Harpoons
- Battering Ram
- Scrolls
- Maps
- Map of the new season
- Astral maps
- Underground maps
- Bars

- Undoing—a frequency weapon, particularly for witchcraft induced frequencies in people, time, and places. Enables angels to shut portals
- Expansion of Ranks
- Booby traps—incendiary devices that will explode or capture an enemy by surprise
- Quietening—enables the quietening of atmospheres where conflict is abounding
- Angel Elixir (or Tonic Elixir)—like an energy drink for angels. It refreshes and brightens them.
- Angel Bread
- Angel Food—translates to comradery among angelic ranks
- Permission to pursue the enemy raiding parties who have been sent to plunder realms
- Scribe Angels[17]
- Listening Devices

In the preceding list, we gave explanation as we knew it where we thought it helpful. The purpose of many of the aforementioned items can be ascertained, yet some items we do not understand at this time.

One of the best ways we can assist our angels in their work for us is to pray in the spirit. Paul gave hints to the

---

[17] Scribe Angels are recording angels that maintain records of various things.

power of praying in tongues in 1 Corinthians 14, where he taught on the subject. In verse 8, Paul refers to a trumpet. That word seems out of place, but it was a marker pointing you to Numbers 10:9, where the trumpet is described as a means of directing the troops in battle. One purpose of speaking in tongues is to direct angelic troops in battle.

Tongues also builds a framework for revelation to abide in, so build your framework large. Do you want a utility shed or a warehouse? Speak in tongues accordingly.

Speaking in tongues does more than you are aware of, as your angels hearken to your words and flow with them in the dimensional spaces that speaking in tongues creates. It is as though when we speak in tongues, it creates pathways in the spirit realm for our angels to traverse through so they can get where they need to go to faster. You might describe it as a worm hole.

Speaking in tongues enables the angels and is a way of co-partnering with them in taking care of issues that arise. Paul further instructed us not to forbid the speaking with tongues,[18] which is solid advice, considering what we have learned just now.

Heaven says to request of the Father greater wisdom for the use of your communication devices and be aware

---

[18] 1 Corinthians 14:39

that spying and infiltrating through deceptive means is at work by the enemy.

Therefore, praying in tongues is so important. Praying in the spirit language is a communication of code that the devil often cannot decipher. Since Satan cannot decipher it because it is of the Holy Spirit, this manner of language is important to be spoken in your atmosphere consistently and whenever prompted by the Spirit of the Lord.

What you need to understand is the spirit of the Lord will prompt you to speak in tongues in advance of a thing that you cannot see yet, and as a measure of protection for what you may walk into. *It is a roadmap for the solution, resolution, and introduction of the solution into the physical plane—into the physical realm.* The solution comes through your mouth.

He dwells in you and often needs to speak, directing the spirit realm and what it contains in mysterious ways, far greater than your understanding. If you do not speak in tongues, ask the Lord for this gift.

Chapter 7
Angels in Captivity

We had discussed some of the details covered in this encounter in previous chapters but not all our questions were answered. Heaven had some more information for us.

Why are angels captured by realms of darkness?

Angels, as servants of those called to be heirs of salvation, are at the behest of their human even before a person accepts Jesus as Lord and Savior. In that time of their life (BC—Before Christ) the angels are in a vulnerable position. The human can begin to seek after dark ways and dark knowledge and go down dark paths. As these Personal Angels accompany them, workers of darkness can capture them, so they are unable to complete their assignment to the person. This has happened more often than people realize.

If you were to look at some of the people you know whose life is in absolute chaos, it is likely a result of:

(1) the dark roads they may have traveled,

(2) the fact that their angel is in captivity and unable to assist them as they are designed to do.

I learned recently while bringing those with slavery in their generations into freedom, that often, if the person was in captivity to slavery, their angel also was in captivity to some degree and had to be brought to freedom as well.

Not All Angels War

Many have taught that all angels do warfare, but that is not necessarily true. Some angels do, but not all. Guardian and Personal Angels would be involved in warfare like a human guardian might seek to protect the one in their care, but they are not equipped for a large degree of warfare. Angelic hosts who specialize in warfare can accomplish those tasks, but they typically need to be invited to engage.

Hearkening to the Voice of the Lord

As you know, and have been made to understand, angels hearken to the voice of the Lord.[19] Believers carry the voice of the Lord. One way that can be accomplished is by speaking in tongues, for then you are speaking directly to God.[20] Angels understand what has been spoken and heed the instructions given as one prays in the spirit and in tune with the spirit. You have been

---

[19] Psalm 103:20
[20] 1 Corinthians 14:2

taught that as a believer prays in tongues, he/she is directing the traffic of the angels in warfare. Much warfare from the enemy has been against tongues through the last century and even beyond. The enemy had some success in snuffing out the gift of tongues from the life of the believer and the church, but it has returned in recent years, and those who will embrace this gift with boldness and directness, will accomplish much via the words of their mouth.

Raiding Parties

When the forces of darkness perceive that a person's realm is a threat, they often send raiding parties into that realm to create havoc. It is in times like these that the Personal Angel might be overwhelmed and suffer defeat at the hands of the raiding party. Since most people have never commissioned their angels to do anything, and have not properly equipped their angel, the angel can be defeated in these situations. Often, the angel is taken captive or bound in some way so they cannot fulfill their duties effectively.

Determining Captivity & Rescuing Angels

When a person's angel is in captivity, determining this is simple. Ask that the angel(s) come forth. If they have not come forth in a matter of a few moments and your spirit does not discern that they are engaged in conflict and cannot come, simply ask of Holy Spirit at that point if they are in captivity. If they are, then request access to the Court of Angels and request that a rescue party be sent to redeem them from their captivity. When praying for another person, it may be required of you to repent on behalf of the person for any actions or words that contributed to their angel's captivity. Once the request for the rescue party has been made, then you can request backup to be sent to the person whose angel is captive. This backup will come from angels of the next higher ranking of angels so that no lack of experience, understanding, or strategy occurs. These angels will often be able to fill out what was missing in the person's life.

Once the backup angels are released to the person, commission them to take their posts to secure the realm of the person you are working with. Ask them if they have need of anything to fulfill their duties. Then, ask of the Father for those items they mention to you. This co-laboring creates a synergy in the realms of Heaven and in the earth between the parties involved.

Once the angel has been rescued, it is likely they will need a time of restoration, especially if they have been in captivity. Request a time of restoration for them. Once granted, the angel will be taken to a place of recovery. Periodically you can check on their recovery status. The length of time required for restoration varies from angel to angel and by the amount of injury they have endured. Once they are deemed sufficiently recovered to return to duty, they will be sent back. At that time, it is helpful for the human to commission them to their post and to guard their realm, also requesting of the Father anything they may need to fulfill their tasks.

A.W.O.L. Angels

Because men have not understood these workings of angels, many angels have been unengaged in their earthly duties. Just as humans sometimes do, they get bored with their tasks (or lack thereof) and seek more exciting things to do. In some cases, they wander, and in other cases they wander so severely as to go A.W.O.L. (Absent Without Leave). They have abandoned their post. When that occurs, the A.W.O.L. angel needs to be brought on trial in the Court of Adjudication for Angelic Hosts for their dereliction of duty. This is a court specializing in correction of wrong behavior of angels assigned to duties. Just as your earthly military would try a soldier with Dereliction of Duty because they went AWOL from their posts, so does Heaven work similarly.

The assignment of angels is a serious matter to Heaven and to the Father. At times angels request a change of assignment due to the frustrations of working with the humans to which they have been assigned. Sometimes this is granted and sometimes the change of assignment is not granted. It is up to the Court of Adjudication to determine that.

The expectation of one's Personal Angel to handle every assault against the realms of person's life is naïve. Much of the theology concerning the angelic hosts is misguided and focuses on the weaknesses of some and not on the strength of the whole of the angelic hosts. As you know of Clarence from the movie "It's a Wonderful Life" with Jimmy Stewart, his bumbling created quite a mess for the star of the movie. The angelic hosts of Heaven are not so inept as Clarence was depicted in that movie. Other movies and television series have also depicted angels in unkind and inaccurate lights as well. Much marketing is geared to show angels to only be cherubic in nature and only interested in affecting one's romantic life. Again, these are all inaccurate depictions of these mighty hosts of Heaven.

Guardian Angels and Personal Angels are not generally equipped for heavy warfare situations; however, that is simply because they serve a different function than Angels of Warfare serve. There are instances in Scripture that describe the different tasks of Angels as Messengers, Angels of Healing, Angels of Harvest, Gathering Angels, and many more. These specialties serve mankind well.

Those angels appointed to be Guardian Angels are assigned for the duration of the person's existence—not merely their existence on the earth. The angels remain assigned to the individual throughout eternity. This goes far beyond what humans have long thought, but nevertheless, the assignment of an angel to a human is a long-term assignment. These angels have a longing to be able to fellowship and cooperate with their human assignment in a myriad of ways, not the least of which is to converse with them in the human's everyday existence.

Learning to Listen

Outside of the voice of one's own spirit, and the voice of Holy Spirit, the Personal Angel wants to be the next dominant voice in their life. Most humans, however, do not know the voice of their own spirit. Few have understood it, and few have taught about how to do so, but it is an essential skill to learn. It is the voice you hear when all other noise fades away.

As Holy Spirit said to me recently, "you chose to engage with me a while ago and you and I have been in conversation for some time now. As you noticed, it was your intent to engage with me that enabled it to occur with ease. Once you made the transition into the realms of Heaven to engage with me, the conversation immediately began to flow. You did not have to "prime the pump" so to speak to begin the conversation, it simply began. In the same way your Personal Angel wants to engage with you in conversation. He is eager to begin the exchange with you. He has much that he can share to aid you in your journey on the earth. You need not make it difficult to begin to engage. Make a declaration of your mouth to your angel that you wish to engage and begin the engagement." Again, Heaven makes it easy, religion has made it hard.

Angels in Recovery

A short time ago, we engaged Heaven to check in on the status of Ezekiel, our ministry angel. When he appeared, it was clear that he had experienced some rough battles and needed some recovery time. We were guided to request that he be taken to a place of restoration and that backup angels be sent to take his place. Although Ezekiel could not be perceived, the presence of two other angels could be perceived. These were Ezekiel's backups, and they began to explain that things are unfolding and are going to get better. We are pleased to be the backups for Ezekiel. Ezekiel has been on the front lines for a long time and needed this rest. We were informed that Ezekiel was mending quickly. (When this angel said rest, this is not rest like we know rest. It is of an entirely different flavor. It does not come with the same connotation.)

Suddenly, we were standing in the Court of Angels speaking to the attendant where we requested some things for the backup angels and for Ezekiel, the ministry angel and his commanders and their ranks.

One of the backup angels was engaged in rewriting the strategy for the orders for the commanders and ranks for better strategy. The other angel began looking at what looked like a video. He was checking on places around the globe, under the earth and outside the earth. What he was viewing seemed dimensional, yet he was looking geographically, and he was scanning throughout the earth. He was looking out and he was passing through all kinds of videos, spot cameras, and checking them one after the other very quickly.

He stopped on a spot in Saudi Arabia indicating a person affiliated with the ministry who needed back up. He saw one in Florida that needed attention and one in one of the northern states in the United States—Michigan. These needs were noted and taken care of by the dispatch of angelic help to these persons.

One of the angels began unveiling that a few trade routes that were being disputed. This attack was coming from the enemy. Angels were also dispatched to handle that issue.

"Can you tell us if it has a specific person in this case?" we asked. They confirmed who it was and that it involved choices the person was making. The person was being faced with a choice to expand their engagement with us, and it was being disputed by darkness. We were instructed that more angelic activity was needed for that person. They disclosed that they were sending two angels there to guard the gate related to that trade route.

We asked, "Can you talk to me more about the realm of the gate?"

On that realm are continual bombardments. We were told to think of that realm as an outpost, but it was not solidly manned. We would request a small contingent of angels (five or six) to accomplish securing that gate of that realm in Saudi Arabia.

"I hear the word Sarasota and it just feels vacant," Donna explained.

The angel explained that the Sarasota gate was not current. It had been shifting. Donna could see a padlock that was open on the gate and the angel simply closed the padlock locking it.

He was describing a gate related to Sarasota that formerly was open and simply needed to be closed which he did for us.

He explained that some of these challenges were what he referred to as a time realm dimensional interrupt.

"Does Ezekiel have access to this same information that you just looked through?" we asked.

"Yes. He has access to it, but when angels get weak, their ability to see to all necessary things diminishes, just as it does with humans," the angel replied.

He began to explain what happened with Ezekiel. "If you have ranks and you have someone in your rank that has been taken out, you don't bring a lesser rank up, you bring a higher rank down because that higher ranked angel already has the knowhow. They have already passed those tests to be at the higher rank. He explained that he and the other angel are a higher-ranking angel who have stepped down to cover for Ezekiel. The reason they can do that is because they are a higher-ranking angel. When you asked me if Ezekiel had access to this, yes, he does have access to this and that it is his present work, but having been weakened, he was not able to perform it."

Assisting Your Angel

"What could we have done that would have assisted him, speak in tongues?" we inquired.

"That was probably the best thing that you could do. Your tongues do more than you are aware as your angels hearken to it and flow with it in the dimensional spaces that speaking in tongues creates," he explained.

Seeking to explain what she was seeing, Donna described, "It looks like when we speak in tongues, it creates wormholes that angels can go through quicker and faster to get to the places they need."

Tongues also serve as a way of commanding angels by directing traffic, so to speak. It is a trumpet sound that Paul mentioned in 1 Corinthians 14:8 where he was alluding to Number 10:9 where trumpets were used to direct the armies in battle. Paul's use of it in 1 Corinthians was a pointer.

Speaking in tongues also is an enabling, a directing, and an assisting. It is a co-partnering. We cannot afford to neglect it. It always accomplishes more than we know.

Chapter 8
Angels & Relationships

Heaven uses all kinds of imagery to explain things to us. This time the image was of a Rolodex—a popular item for storing names and addresses in days gone by. Now, our cell phones serve that purpose, but Heaven used the image, explaining that this Rolodex represents relationships to the ministry.

Heaven explained that we have relationships that need to go, and relationships that need to be solidified from heavenly trade. Some relationships need to be guarded, and some need to be built.

We trade from Heaven with the Father *for the benefit of* and *from the benefit of beneficial relationships*—a formal network that strengthens. Relationships are things that angels assist with and, because of that, we simply need to request that Ezekiel assist us.

Ezekiel began to explain, "I am a relationship arranger. I have access to this Rolodex. I know what is pending to leave, what needs to stay, and what needs to be enriched for the ministry to carry out the purpose of the Father as an ambassador of the kingdom. I can do some rearranging on your behalf and while I carry this charge out in the background, sometimes there are key times where you will ask me to perform this duty on your behalf with specificity.

Lydia interjected explaining, "You have a moment of opportunity where you can ask Ezekiel and his team to finalize the order of the relationships that LifeSpring needs to have. This has already begun happening for you as we have been working together, but a new installment of additions, subtractions, and a clearing up of some things is needed—and that's what we can accomplish together today."

Ezekiel explained, "This is like a commissioning of me to order your relationships afresh."

Charge to Ezekiel

Lydia shared, "It is not hard. It is simple. You just say to Ezekiel, the angel of the ministry of LifeSpring International Ministries:

We commission and charge you to your duty of relationship order and ordering relationships for LifeSpring that will bring the benefit of the Father and the blessing of the Father.

We ask you to circumvent the realms and bring these in.

We ask you to solidify those that are in our relationship base with whom the Father is pleased.

We ask you to transfer out all unnecessary relationships or those relationships causing theft of resources, time, and finances.

We ask you also Ezekiel to clean out debris from those relationships. If the relationship has an ending time in Heaven's scrolls, we request that you abide by the Father's Word in this and bring these relationships to finality and to an end.

We bless those who have walked with the ministry for a time and release them with blessing to their next.

We ask Ezekiel to perform the act of sentry at the gates of the realm of LifeSpring International Ministries that no relationships that are not written by the Father or according to divine will be allowed access to the realm as either customer, client, friend, those with employee status, or those aligned as students.

Basically, we are asking Ezekiel to swab the decks and to bring into right order the tightened relationships that our Father desires this ministry to have. Clear out the old, bring in the new, and help us establish with solidarity the relationships of people that are already connected to us."

Ezekiel says, "What you're basically asking me to do is to 'spit shine' the relationships at the ministry."

"Yes," we replied.

It was suggested that I verbally agree with all of that, so I said, "I agree with all of that."

More About Relationships

Stepping into the flow of revelation that you need is easier than you realize. You have already prepared yourself. For example, today with the ministry's Platinum members, have them step in. Let one of them lead the way. Keep building the relationship with those I highlight. I have things planned for that relationship and Heaven has even greater plans. Many times, relationships can be brought closer for you.

Remember, your angel is a relationship builder. They can build relationships out of what seems to be nothing and create a strength and trust in them that can allow it to be sustained for long periods of time. They can help you in strengthening relationships you have so you can do what is needed to be done.

When two people have in their heart for the Lord to build the relationships Heaven desires, a cooperation can begin between their angel and your angel. This will strengthen the relationships. Each person's angel can aid you in knowing what bonds need to be released in the human's life. Many have questioned what they have heard in that regard, not realizing the information was coming via their angel to them because of a purposing of hearts to do so. The purposing of hearts is like an intent. It is essentially the same. Intent is needed because it creates a flow of focus concerning the subject of the intent. Without intent, little can happen, but with intent, much can be accomplished in one's life.

Jesus talked about focusing your intent, He just did not use those words. He said in Mark 11 that if you will "say to this mountain." It was not to just any mountain, but to a specific mountain. That is intent. That is focus. Just as you have weaponry that can focus on a particular thing a great distance away, you also have weapons that scatter their shots in a larger area. Most believers use a shotgun approach to their faith, and the exercise of their faith, rather than a laser guided approach to a particular mountain—a particular thing—a particular result. Focus of intent is key. It draws your faith reservoir from all quarters to a particular thing, so that thing can be impacted by the release of faith. You will do this today on specific things, but regarding relationships, you have several dynamics in play.

1. The intent of the heart of multiple parties to have a deeper relationship according to their scrolls.
2. The determination to obey leadings from Heaven (we will talk about that more soon) regarding relationships.
3. The willingness to obey Heaven regarding praying and blessing the life of the other party.
4. The release of bonds according to the needs of the relationship and the other party is key here.

5. The instruction of your angel to cooperate with the other party's angel to facilitate the relationship.
6. Remember to instruct your angel to cooperate with the Bond Registry Angels as they minister the requested bonds.

Doing these things, following these steps, will aid the relationship building. Request your angel to build the relationships in your life according to your scroll. They will begin to pull out the relationships for the season you are in. You do not need winter relationships in the middle of summer. You may have some camaraderie, but it will not be what it should be. You want the relationships to be in season. Seasons are important—naturally and otherwise.

Chapter 9
Messenger Angels

Donna and I had just engaged Heaven to discover what was on our agenda for that day. Shortly afterward, Ezekiel, the chief angel over our ministry, appeared with a large messenger bag slung over his shoulder. He had a message for us, but this time the message was about messages and Messenger Angels. Over the next few pages, I am simply going to share what Ezekiel shared as it relates to our ministry.

He began, "A messenger bag is for messages."

"Are you ready to learn how to send a message in the spirit?" he asked.

"Yes," was our reply to him.

In past engagements with Ezekiel, he had proven a very capable teacher and today was to be no different.

Sending Messages in the Spirit

Messenger Angels carry messages. In scripture, we can read where angels are sent from the Father to various places and individuals with messages. At times, you have experienced a flow of the Holy Spirit where understanding and knowledge flow directly from the Holy Spirit to your spirit, so that you know how to minister.

If you have been following our teachings on the Tuesday night mentoring group, you have learned how to receive messages by stepping into the realms of Heaven to receive messages like from the bond registry or Help Desk or things like that. You also can make use of the angels assigned to your ministry.

Messages can be delivered in the spirit by spirit beings who are assigned to you and working on your team. Ezekiel said to us, "I and my ranks commanders and ranks are on your team. We are team members, and you need to start looking at us as team members, so when the ministry has a need, you can send an email or you can send an angel—yes, you can commission an angel, one of my ranks—to deliver the message.

One certain type of angel is known as Messenger Angels. We can release them to carry messages in the spirit realm that we normally would have to deliver ourselves by other means. The ministry had been seeing an ever-increasing number of emails that was getting harder to manage and had become quite time consuming. We were learning this with the end goal being to see the influx of emails go from Niagara Falls to a trickling brook.

We can come into agreement that Ezekiel has Couriers and Messenger Angels. We can ask that messages be taken in the spirit to people. We were told we would have to learn this and learn how this works.

Ezekiel explained, "The reason this has not worked for those who have not understood this, is because most Christians do not know that messages can continually be brought to them and they can understand these messages." Ezekiel reminded Donna of a recent event when her grandbaby's angel came and stood in front of her. It was a Messenger Angel that Donna received—that angel had a message and a purpose. The angel was reporting a situation to Donna, so Donna immediately commissioned the angel to deal with it. Donna was able to do that because she caught it. Ezekiel said, "Imagine if that angel was simply standing around waiting to be noticed and Donna had not been paying attention or was unable to discern the angel's presence.

This is what Christianity has not understood because the Body of Christ has been so accustomed to looking in the natural, not the supernatural. Yes, as soon as you discern the supernatural, you see many Messenger Angels, and then the Messenger Angel base can begin to be activated.

Amail vs. Email

Ezekiel continued, "The reason I'm talking to you about this is because Lydia has been talking to you about the email situation and because this is kind of how it works. Naturally, you have email, but in the supernatural you have angels (Amail). An angel can bring you a vision. An angel can bring you a knowing. An angel can bring you an understanding. An angel can bring you a revelation and an angel can bring you the face of a person.

Once you discern their presence, the second thing to do is question Holy Spirit, "This angel has brought this to me, what do I do with this?" The function of Holy Spirit dwelling within you is to help with wisdom, counsel, and to assist your engagement with the seven spirits of God about what to do with the message that has just come to you.

There is a network of Messenger Angels that want to operate much more swiftly and with much more ease to assist the Body of Christ. They want to relieve the pressures of lack of communication or excessive unnecessary communication.

The first church did this all the time. This is why when Peter showed up at the door after being released from prison by the angels, they thought it was Peter's angel bringing a message, and not Peter himself who was standing at the door of the house.

The early church had a strong knowing of these concepts. We must be aware that plenty of warfare exists around Courier Angels—the Messenger Angels that are sent out with messages.

Most Christians think they are only sent out with messages from the Father. We must rethink that. Messenger Angels are sent out on behalf of the saints—those whose faces are turned to God, those who have His light, those who are utilizing their five spiritual senses. Messenger Angels respond to the five spiritual senses and they can use the five spiritual senses to bring you the message that they are needing to bring you. But some of the messages are from other saints. They are not from the godhead; however, they can be. Jesus sends his angels; the Father sends his angels and Holy Spirit has angels that He sends.

Network of Messenger Angels

A whole angel network exists whose purpose is to go back and forth between the ministries, between the nations, between the dimensions and places in the realms of Heaven. Messenger Angels come from those places. Sometimes you have received a Messenger Angel that has been sent to you to tell you there is a court case so that you appear in court. Sometimes, from the realms of Heaven, there has been something going on in a Council Room that you have needed to appear in or know about, and an angel has been sent—not from the Father,

Son, and Holy Spirit—but from the cloud of witnesses and the angelic beings that come out of the realms of Heaven into the natural realm, so that it goes well with you in both realms.

"Do you see this messenger bag?" Ezekiel asked. "I need it to be full, so that I can distribute the messages to my ranks, and they can go on their way." He instructed, "You do not have to go through me personally. You can call one of my ranks and ask a Messenger Angel of the ranks, assigned to the ministry to be released to deal with the situation or to impart information, knowledge, and understanding about a thing to a person.

Abusing the Privilege

Ezekiel continued, "Just like in other things, when they understand this, humanity, in their infancy will abuse this. The risk of abuse of Messenger Angels is high. There are some Messenger Angels in Heaven who do not want to deal with the body of Christ in her infancy regarding this because they risk such harm, and they risk capture. They are created to do this, but they are aware of the risks as they deal with the bride of Christ and the humanity of Christ body on earth in her infancy of relearning this." Ezekiel says, "Trust me, this is a relearning. This information has been in the earth realm for a long time."

Ezekiel then showed some Celtic saints and other saints from early church times. They dealt with this.

They understood this. The early church fathers understood this too.

Receipt of the Message is the Goal

The Messenger Angel can be equipped and thanked and commended. A Messenger Angel can be given elixir and angel food. When a Messenger Angel comes and delivers a message, **the receipt of the message is what they are after**. They are not after the delivering of the message, they are after the receipt of the message.

Just prior to this meeting with Ezekiel, an angel appeared from one of our staff members. Although initially Donna thought it was that person's Personal Angel, it was a Messenger Angel sent by the staff persons angel with a message. Donna acknowledged the angel, received the message and, in turn, gave instructions to be taken back to our team member to assist them in a matter. Once the messenger returned to the team members angel, their angel would have information and instruction to assist them.

Never out of a teaching moment, Donna looked out the window of her office and saw a large raven who looked rather haggard. She immediately discerned that it was a manifestation of a spy sent to spy on Donna and what was occurring. She immediately dispatched it from her property.

She realized that she needed to pause and take care of something. Donna had just returned from a short vacation and, prior to leaving, had set angels to protect her home and property.

Donna began, "Father, I thank you for the angels that guarded my house and my property against every access and dimensional access point while I was gone. Now that I am back, in Jesus name, I commend these angels to you that guarded my home and the portal that is here. I ask that these angels be served angel elixir and angel food and angel bread. I ask that they be given assistance and backup and I ask for new angels to come and to help keep the portal open here and to guard the property and every dimensional access point against evil, darkness, and unrighteousness."

As she was praying she suddenly felt the influx of the new angels, so she continued, "I thank you Father for the new angels that are here and I loose them to their work—to capture every spy of darkness, and where those spies of darkness have crossed a line, to punish them with immediate punishment in Jesus' name. I also ask the new angels that have arrived for the increase of the water flow that comes out of Heaven into this portal in Jesus' name. I ask for a widening of the waterfall of living water flowing from Heaven."

She immediately saw a gate and asked, "Holy Spirit. Why do I see a gate? Do I need to reopen the gate?"

Speaking to the angels that had come she said, "I instruct the newer, fresh angels that have come to patrol the realm of the property and guard my realms against every dimensional access point. Now that I am back in my geographical place, I instruct you to open the gate and to perform sentry duty and to only allow access through the gate of the property realm, and my realm, and this spiritual realm those Messenger Angels from Lord Sabaoth—any messengers of the King of glory. You can let the Angels of the Bond Registry in, and all angels delivering messages from other saints, and you are to deny access to spies of darkness, demons, and those who are plotting against me and my family and this ministry in the name of Jesus."

Donna explained, "When I left, I asked angels to guard everything here at my home. Ezekiel explained that it was like those angels shuttered the house and closed the gate. Donna realized that when she got back, she had to open it up again.

What the Messenger Angels are waiting for is a recognition

They are often waiting for a verbal receipt of the message they have brought. The verbal response of a believer in the physical realm is the pathway through which this exchange happens. It happens through verbal frequency, which is the crossing between the two realms from the spirit realm to the earth realm and forms a bridge. The verbal frequency of "I receive what you have. Thank you for bringing it," is simple enough to form the manifestation of its receipt into the physical realm.

You are a portal of the kingdom. Yet, if you are a portal of the kingdom, how does it manifest in the natural? It manifests through a sound frequency. Sound frequency waves are one of the more contested things in the earth realm. The enemy wants to fill or replace the frequencies in the earth with his own frequencies and cause unsuspecting Christians to release wrong sound frequencies.

The body of Christ is growing up in this because the individual members are beginning to realize how important the sound frequencies are. There are two things going on:

(1) There is the shutting down of sound frequencies from the body of Christ where they are being distracted and not saying what Heaven is saying. They are not saying what angels are saying. They are not saying the messages that angels are bringing. They are not saying the revelation that is flowing.

(2) They are not saying it verbally because some of them have been taught that you have to pray quietly and privately in your brain or in your mind, when you need to be praying out loud and talking out loud. You are speaking to the unseen, but you are speaking to the seen as well.

Ezekiel explained, "I'm just in a different realm, but you and I communicate by sound frequencies. You are hearing my frequency, but when you talk to me out loud, you are pulling what I am saying to you into this natural world, into this realm. The enemy has told the church they can only pray quietly in their mind, so they never open their mouth.

Freeing the chains off people's mouths and tongues is important for their spiritual growth. Therefore, speaking and praying in tongues is so important. It is a representation of the spirit coming through your frequency into the natural realm.

Speaking to angels must be done verbally. Many of your students are speaking to angels or attempting to speak to angels through the mind. This is not impossible, but it is not the designated manner. Speaking to angels out loud is what we need, especially if a message has been brought to you, that Messenger Angel wants to hear the receipt of what you have been told. Just repeat out loud what the angel told you. That is form of receipt. You could speak to the angel directly and say, "I perceive you. I hear what you are saying, and I agree with it." That is another form of receipt. Or you could just say, "I don't know who you are, but I receive what you brought in the name of Jesus." That is a form of receipt.

First Things First

Where Christians get in a mess is, they have not done the first things first so that they can receive a messenger from the hosts of Heaven. They have not sent their angels to patrol their realm and make sure that only those who were coming from Yahweh are getting in. If you have not done that foundational work first and yet you are receiving every spirit that walks in and presents itself to you, you are going to receive wrong spirits.

This is where the body of Christ operates in immaturity and infancy and where they have not grown up in the foundation of who they are in Christ and their ability to do these things—hence, they are just receiving all kinds of things.

It must line up with the Word. It must line up with the sense of Holy Spirit resonating a similar frequency within you. The reason this has not been happening is because Christians have been taught to fear these messages that are coming from Heaven and many of them have not cleansed their mind and are not feeding themselves on the revelatory flow of Heaven. They are not feeding themselves on the word of God. They are feeding themselves on so many things that are not of God.

You have to know what you are feeding on and you have to understand that you have been working with the godhead to mature, always focusing on the King, always looking to hear what the Father is saying. That intimate relationship of having those basic things in place prevents you from mishaps and the receiving of a wrong spirit. Angels help you with this. Your Personal Angels help you with this. Heaven explained, "Angels can do many things in the unseen realm, but you need to tell your people this. They are present to help you so that you can receive new messages."

Ezekiel began to give another example. He asked, "If you release a Messenger Angel to someone and they have not done the things that they need to do to receive the message, then the chances of her receiving the message are not your fault. It is their fault. It is not the Messenger Angel's fault. It is the person's fault because they were not ready to receive." He continued, "The mercy and grace of Heaven is such that angels are able to wait until they catch that person in a moment where they can receive."

The teaching of how to receive the Messenger Angels is also the teaching of how to remain in Christ Jesus— how to abide in him, dwell in his presence and heart, hearken to the Holy Spirit, and cultivate intimacy with the Father.

"So how will we put that into practice with something right now?" I asked Donna.

"What about J* (one of our staff members)?"

I request a Messenger Angel assigned to the ministry, LifeSpring International Ministries to take a message to J*.

J*, we honor your work for the ministry, we honor your diligence for it. We understand the tension that you feel between your different roles and we release grace to you and oil of anointing to flow in between your roles without pressure, but with peace—the King's peace, the Prince of peace. We release this vile of oil. We ask you angel to release this vial of oil to J* for those reasons. We ask you to anoint J* with peace, grace, ease, respect, and honor for what he does with the ministry. We release you to take that to J* in Jesus' name. Thank you.

Although our spiritual cups were full Ezekiel was not quite done. He pointed out an event that had occurred with Donna the day before while returning from the airport. Someone had texted her with an "emergency". Donna knew in her spirit that the situation was not an "emergency" but merely a situation. She did not respond by text to the friend but began speaking to her spirit and asked angels to minister to her spirit.

Ezekiel pointed out that what she had done was a form of releasing a Messenger Angel to someone.

It is likely you have experienced this more than you may realize. May we grow up into these understandings as we learn to rely more on Heaven than on the earth.

Chapter 10
Cooperating with the Angel of Currency

During our first meeting with the Currency Angel, he was shown to us as a being who had the currencies of all nations covering his clothes and embedded in him like tattoos. He stood with Lydia waiting for us. We needed to know more, and Heaven was happy to oblige. Moments later Ezekiel would help us out. We began with a question, "Do you work with the Currency Angel?"

Ezekiel replied, "I certainly do. I am aware of him and his presence and my ranks often accompany him. He is the type of angel that sometimes needs protection from warring entities. I am aware of his light trail and movement in earth realm and yes, he is a unique angel.

The Father has many wonderful angels. They respond to their duty with veracity and ferociousness. We often must employ booby traps to help this angel on his path as he is about his duty. Nets are often used as well, to deal with the small creatures like mice or a fox among the vines who intend to steal the hidden wealth of the Father and that of the saints. That is why we accompany the Currency Angel on his forays and as he goes about his duties. He uses our help and other assistance from assigned angels to accomplish his duties."

Speaking to me, Ezekiel said, "Ron, if you sense a slowdown in the equation of increase release and needed increase it is probably because the Currency Angel has run into trouble and we can dialogue and help you with that. We can check in on him for you. If you ever sense that is happening, let us work together."

He continued, "Other angels are like the Currency Angel, but they do not bring currency. They do not trade in currency. They trade in the other things that you consider wealth, as well as things like relationships, offspring, and other intangible things that you may not consider to be wealth. It is a mystery, but there are many realms these angels are designed to operate in and do operate in. The Currency Angel is a type of Gathering Angel."

Donna asked, "Am I able to ask my angels to engage the Angel of Relationship for another person?"

Ezekiel replied, "I can ask my angels to check on them and see if there is a need or if there's trouble. You know how you have seen angels trapped and captured? Well, some of these angels get trapped and captured and they need Warring Angels like myself and my ranks to free them. Some Warring Angels are just that—Warrior Angels. Some are like me who have a rank of Commanding Angel. I command numerous things, not just the war aspect, but expansion of destiny over the thing that I have as my duty, which in this case is LifeSpring."

Chapter 11
Court of Decrees
and the Court of Angels

We had become aware of some attacks against the ministry and decided to engage Heaven for answers. We accessed the Court of Records and began to gaining some understanding

The angelic assistant in the Office of the Registry informed us that the ungodly bonds were being supplied against us by the Court of Accusation in the Court of Hell. We had stirred up the wrath of the Courts of Hell from the ambushes and the booby traps we had placed before. Holy Spirit was admonishing us to stand strong. Hell will get tired of this after a while and will look for easier prey we were told.

Then Holy Spirit said, "Loose angels to discomfort the Court of Hell and to plunder hidden realms where darkness lies. Use the Court of Angel's warriors that are Snipers, Bounty Hunters, Ambushers, and Fire Starters." Then he said, "Release the arrows of the Lord— the

Arrows of the Lord, Arrows of Fire, and Arrows of Light." Then, we were instructed to go immediately to the Court of Decrees concerning this request.

Accessing the Help Desk of the Courts of Heaven, we made our request, "We would like to acquire someone to help us access the Court of Decrees to request a royal decree regarding the loosing of angels."

An angel came and led us onto an elevator. We arrived and upon entry to this room we were asked to sign in and put the date of our visit. We were given a preliminary form to complete regarding our request. The preliminary form had to be submitted and approved by the Court of Decrees. Once a decree had preliminary approval, it would then go to receive a time stamp (indicating the time for its release in the earth).

We were instructed to rely on the unction of the Holy Spirit when filling out the form. So we made an application to the Court of Decrees for a loosing of angelic warriors on behalf of LifeSpring International Ministries and that any of the Class of Warriors known as Snipers, Bounty Hunters, Ambushers, and Fire Starters be released against the Courts of Hell to the hidden realms where darkness lies. We request angelic armor to accompany these warriors being the Arrows of the Lord, the Arrows of Flaming Fire, and the Arrows of Light. We request this by royal decree and agree with the divine timing of Yahweh. We then signed the form.

An angel took the preliminary form to begin the process of the paperwork and another angel led us into a court area where we were being seated. It appeared to be part of the gallery except that we were on the main floor. We were waiting our turn. Many people were in the same room with us.

Ezekiel suddenly joined us saying he did not want to miss this. Then, it was our turn before the court.

We were being asked, "Are you here to represent LifeSpring International Ministries?"

"Yes," we replied. An attendant of the court then began to read what was on the preliminary form.

A court clerk began checking a database and found some pertinent information that agreed with our request.

We were asked if we would agree for the immediate release of the decree and we replied, "We would be in agreement with swift retribution."

We then received a scroll. The assistant recommended we notice that the scroll was not sealed meaning it was available for immediate release.[21] With the receiving of the scroll, we were finished in the Court of Decrees.

Next Ezekiel escorted us to the Court of Angels where he presented the recent royal decree that we had

---

[21] Scrolls that have a future timing are sealed (see Daniel 12:4).

received. Since it was for immediate release Ezekiel pointed our attention to what was then happening in the Court of Angels.

Angels in warrior dress came in and Ezekiel had them turn around to show us their quivers. We saw a massive arrow.

"Is that the Arrow of the Lord?" we asked. It looked like a massive gold arrow about three to four feet long. With it was the flaming arrow which appeared as if it were coated with gunpowder. Then we saw the Arrows of Light which had a liquid appearance.

"It is a frequency. That is why it looks liquid," an angel explained.

Then, the Warrior Angels left on their mission. Asking Ezekiel if he had ever done what they were about to do, he replied that he had not, but he had heard of their exploits and he knows they are mighty in God because they never fail.

With that completed, we left the Court of Angels to turn to our next task. Curious for more information about what we had just experienced we approached the Help Desk of the Courts of Heaven and said, "We are here looking for information about the protocol where Holy Spirit leads us to pray that the angels of the Lord would discomfort the Courts of Hell and release angels to plunder hidden realms."

Someone began to explain, "The system that works through the Court of Angels operates out of paperwork that is distributed from the other Courts of Heaven. Usually when you come to the Court of Angels, you have paperwork or a writ or you have been given an object. These items can come to you from any of the Courts in Heaven with specific instructions for you to come to the Court of Angels for their delivery. Also, at other times, the court work in which you are involved has already releasing paperwork in the background and angels are released to their duty from these actions.

If you were told to loose angels to discomfort hell, you would need to receive the decree for that. So, the Court of Decrees would be where you would go. You would put in an application for the will of God in that situation, and that court would issue a decree accordingly.

What this is doing is combining a threefold cord. It is combining the unction of the Holy Spirit, the intentional will of the saint, and the divine will of the Father. This creates movement in the Court of Decrees and results in both the decree being issued as well as the time that the decree will be released being set. That decree, once issued in the Court of Decrees, can be brought to the Court of Angels. Sometimes these things are done in the background, especially if it is for a future time. If it is for a future time, it is logged into the Court of Angels and will be taken care of as angels step in to perform their duty on behalf of the Lord. However, some decrees are of a nature that you would be given the decree and requested to take it personally to the Court of Angels. Sometimes this is to build your faith to see angelic activity take up your decree. At other times it is to expedite things. But Heaven does like for saints to know and to see the activity that is begun at their initiation with Courts of Heaven. This is often why you receive an unction to bring an item or a decree or a piece of paperwork to the Court of Angels. So, if we are going to request specifics (specifically what Holy Spirit requests), we would go to the Court of Decrees."

We asked, "Is there anything else that you can tell us that we might need to know about how it works when we request the discomforting of hell?"

He replied, "I cannot tell you the details because that is reserved for the mysteries of angels, but I can tell you that the angelic realm is deployed swiftly and with might, in full armor array. The angels know where to go because they have already spied out entrance places that are like portals to be used when this type of decree comes. This is like plundering. The plundering of hidden realms is like the activity you have seen when you have entered the Trophy Room of Hell.

When angels plunder Hell, they bring out many stolen objects. They bring out stolen lives and stolen resources and they devastate the enemy on their swift foray into his camp. Angels do this more and more due to the initiation of the saints, and at some point, we reach a moment where we can gain back territory from the enemy. This territory will manifest in the earth realm when land is relieved of its torment and the physical earth receives refreshing. We have done this many times for those moving in these realms and in these operations."

We requested, "Could you talk to us about the Arrows of the Lord, the Arrows of Flaming Fire and the Arrows of Light?"

"These are the equipment of Warrior Angels," he explained. "Often the decree contains a specific detail from Holy Spirit, and it is important to pay attention to them, for this gives the angels legal access to these types of weapons. The Flaming Arrows and Arrows of Light are sent from the Lord by angels. They resemble thunderbolts and they cause a scattering instantaneously in dark realms. The Arrow of the Lord brings confusion and chaos to the enemy's camp. When angels use these arrows of the Lord, they are often able to bring out souls, spirits, and those captured in recesses of darkness who are yet alive on the earth, but through fragmentation have lost their parts to regions of darkness," he continued.

We remembered that when Holy Spirit gave this information, He called it a Core Activity by Royal Decree. "Is that a different type of decree or could you help me understand that?" we asked.

The angel explained, "It is a Kingdom decree that is royal in nature in that it is signed by the King through an ambassadorial channel. That decree came through ambassadorial channels from saints and was initiated by saints. Heaven rejoices at this initiation by the saints to release the weapons of war. The divine will in the decree is like the level of a general over a battlefield who knows the proper time to release specific weapons. The weapons being released according to divine will engage the whole battle plan of the Kingdom realm and therefore the timing for their release in battle is critical. **The saints then, as they initiate these things, must understand that their initial work is at the court level, but the time for the working out of these things are according to the divine will thus making it a Royal Decree.** We would be wise to listen to the Holy Spirit's unction about these things."

With that our instruction and explanation about what we had experienced was over. We had more knowledge to aid us in understanding how to cooperate with Heaven as saints in the earth. May you find much gratification in understanding how to work with decrees and the Court of Decrees as we extend the Kingdom of God in the earth.

Chapter 12
Plundering the Enemies Camp

Our session began with Ezekiel advising us that provision was being released, but the provision trains[22] needed protection. "This provision is from the Father's storehouses, but the delivery of provision has a timing component to it as well, so the delivery and the timing need to be protected as well," Ezekiel explained.

Donna and I immediately issued a charge and commission to Ezekiel:

> *We do charge and commission our angel(s) and their ranks to protect the provision that is coming to us. Protect it on its way. See that what has been slated for release comes to manifestation.*

"Are there weapons that you need for that?" we asked.

In our situation we knew he had maps, but he requested something called guideposts. These are

---

[22] The trains that carry the provision.

recognized by angels. On earth we have traffic signals on thoroughfares. Angels have guideposts and know the markings of the guideposts. We made the request of the Father and Heaven continued in our instruction.

Offensive and Defensive Thinking

Heaven told us that we need to begin to think in terms of offense, not defense, regarding the provision that the Father has for us. Ezekiel was suggesting an offensive stance. He explained, "There is provision that comes based on your giving, your offerings, and your obedience where you see the field that is yours—the ministry's field, where you know you have harvest. It is good to make sure it is protected."

Defense would be where we go to the Court of Reclamation and get back what the enemy has stolen, but offensive measures are about the provision *that is being released*. This comes from the faith that you have that you will be receiving the provision and you are expecting provision. You have done things like make withdrawals from the Finance Department for you provision and you have sown in obedience. It is an offensive stance of protection over the coming prosperity, the release of windfalls, and things like that. We need to learn how to protect it offensively.

Rain from Heaven

We asked Lydia to help us understand.

She began, "It is not as hard as you think. Think of provision as rain from Heaven. The rain is coming, and you must put out your pots to receive it. What happens between the time it leaves the clouds and ends up in the pot? It is that period that needs protecting.

So, we need to charge our angel(s) and their ranks to offensively and aggressively war against the theft or potential theft, derailment, or capture by rerouting of the rain of provision that has been released from the Father to the ministry. This would look like a commissioning of our angels to do this. Ezekiel has maps that he uses for this, as he instructs his ranks to an offensive position, not just defensive.

It is the difference between telling the ranks of angels to protect, but you can also tell them to plunder.

The heavenly host is not looking for a fight from the enemy because they know whose they are and they know the fight is already won, but when the fight comes to them and the enemy makes an attack, you have traditionally stationed your angels to defend what is yours, but...

Now release them also to not only defend what is yours, but to plunder the enemy's camp.

Wouldn't you want that? To plunder is to make Satan pay when he brings the fight and loses.

> Always make him pay by plundering the enemy's camp.

Do not think of camp as singular, *think of the many camps of the enemy from which he attacks you, the staff, the clients, the communication lines, and the provision.* Release your angels to war *defensively,* but *also offensively* to plunder the enemy's camp and gain back what belongs to the Kingdom of God. This would be a warfare activity that Ezekiel is well equipped for. At that point, Ezekiel was demonstrating his agreement with this and his 'can't wait' attitude.

Now Lydia showed a sack of gold and said all the gold and all the silver is the Father's (Haggai 2:8). "The enemy has for eons collected the gold through various means and by various ways, but now is the time to release your angels to plunder the enemy's camps and get back the gold," she explained.

Do you see there is a difference here in the reclamation court where you go for legal means? You can also release angelic activity to plunder the enemy's camp. So, where the enemy has stolen from people who do not even know how to get back it back,

> *Heaven is saying the gold can be retrieved* **by any who will**.

To get the portion of it back is the Father's goal, but if you get it back, it is credited to your action—the action of releasing the angels to the task—in some measure, **no matter who forfeited it.** It is still God's gold. Someone has just got to retrieve it. This falls to the mature saints of God who understand the ways of Yahweh and who are already operating in obedience as true sons.

We asked to be coached in this process and we were told:

It is like a commissioning in which we charge Ezekiel and his ranks so we can capture from the enemy that which has been stolen. Heaven wants to restore to us things that have been stolen—not only from us, but from those that we minister to, from those are associated with the ministry, their families, from their future (or from their past). In every arena, we are plundering to recover all that has been stolen in Jesus' name.

"When the angels recover the bounty, what is the distribution of that?" we asked.

Ezekiel replied, "It comes back to the one who requests it. See your angels as mighty warriors.

Your angels can get what is yours, but they can also get whatever is available.

If you plunder an enemy camp and you see an object that he took from someone you know, you can say, 'I am going to go get that. I see where the enemy took this whole room full of treasure from the kingdom of God, so I claim that too.' That is the plundering of the enemy's camp.

We do not really need to understand or see the distribution. We will just experience it. We will just do this and see what happens."

How to speak to your angel(s):

"We commission you to go to your defensive stance in protection of the provision coming to the ministry, and we also commission you to your offensive stance as well for you and your ranks. We commission you to offensively plunder the enemy's camp, gain what has been stolen and return it to where it needs to go, in Jesus' name."

If you are a Kingdom citizen and the Kingdom has been plundered, you are able to loose angelic hosts to get back whatever the Kingdom lost, whether it is yours or not. This is your right. You have a right to that, but you are also operating as an ambassador of the Kingdom to get back what belongs to the Kingdom and let the King determine what he will do with it. Heaven just wants it back, but Heaven needs sons who will stand in their place and see to it that the plundering of the enemy's camp occurs. Saints—take your place![23]

---

[23] More on this subject is available at the end of Chapter 18 Insights.

Chapter 13
Working with Bond Registry Angels

We ask permission to come back to Help Desk and we are checking it again for LifeSpring International Ministries. We want to know if there is anything on our schedule.

Donna heard the words "bond registry" but was not sure what was being said. She asked for clarification.

"Could someone come and help talk to us about a bond registry and angels?" she asked.

Lydia came and began to explain that she wanted to talk about the revelation in the book regarding the bonds and the bond registry.[24] She gave us a new understanding about the angels and the bond registry.

---

[24] *Releasing Bonds from the Courts of Heaven* (2020) by Dr. Ron M. Horner (LifeSpring Publishing)

In the Court of Records, you have seen assistants who have brought out registries to you, helped you turn pages, and gave you counsel. They are angels assigned to oversee registries of individuals and entities. These angels on duty in the Office of Records are also connected to an army of angels. They take turns working in the bond registry office and carrying out the release of godly bonds requested in the courts, and on bond registries of individuals and entities. By their design, the bond registry is very dear to them. They are grieved when ungodly bonds are assigned, but they are elated when the saints work from courtroom realms to deal with bonds. They are on assignment to enact the outplay of godly bonds that are assigned as courtroom work is done by saints filling bond registries with the godly bonds,

Their activity escalates exponentially because of the filling of bond registry pages with godly bonds. They have a certain type of expression or flavor. They have a particular resonance about them because of their assignment.

These angels are assigned to the bond registry, so they have a particular manner about them. Even their stature and their velocity are really is designed to be related to what they do regarding the bond registry. They are responsible for bringing people the understanding of the bond registry. They are responsible for hearing and receiving the orders of the courts where bonds are released to people, and they engage in the activity of bringing the expression of that bond into a person's life.

For example, a bond of peace released for a person, through the courtroom work of the saints, releases a Bond Registry Angel to the person being prayed for, to bring about peace in that person's realm.

Angelic Ranks

Angels are organized are in ranks like what you would see in an army. There are ranks of these angels and some angels do better than others in their posts and in the outplay of their duties.

So, as the saint prays for the bond registry, an additional understanding of what is being done from the ranks of Heaven's angels will help people understand that they are commanding angels by the courtroom work of the release of godly bonds for individuals, entities, and such. This helps the saint gain a new level of expectation for the playing out of that godly bond. If they are not seeing it or sensing it, or if they sense no angel is assigned to take care of this, then the saint can request of the Father, in the courtroom, that his best angels would be assigned to the carrying out of these released bonds.

Released Bonds

Think of these released bonds in a dimensional manner. They are words on a page in a bond registry, but they are also scrolls handed to the Bond Registry Angels. Personal Angels, such as yours, can interact with these angels, even offering them backup, support, and assistance.

Individuals have Personal Angels or Guardian Angels, and you can instruct your personal or Guardian Angel to receive from or help the Bond Registry Angels. Commission your angel(s) to cooperate with the Bond Registry Angels.

If you're praying for Joe and you are releasing bonds for Joe and you release of a bond of peace for Joe, then you can say to Joe's angel, "Do your work with the Bond Registry Angel to receive what the Bond Registry Angels are bringing for Joe." This is a means of commanding angels. This does not have to be done all the time. It can be done in a revelatory manner—in other words, as you perceive, sense, know, see, hear, or have instruction that a Bond Registry Angel needs help, that's when you would request of the Father that Joe's angel would work with the Bond Registry Angel.

Donna's Friend's Angel

Donna shared a recent encounter with a friend's angel who suddenly showed up. When the friend's angel appeared, she knew whose angel it was. The angel was in need, but her friend did not know how to work with their angel to co-labor with him.

She asked Holy Spirit for instruction on what to request and began making the requests. After a few moments, it was done, and the angel left.

If someone else's angel comes to you, the chances are their angel is on assignment because they are looking for the saints who can help them. They desire the relationship with the saint and, if they do not have the relationship with his person yet, they are hungrily searching for those that they can have relationship with. These angels may need something, or they need a direction, a commission, or a charge, so they may come to you because they know you are sensitive to that and have understanding of these things. Commissioning and charging are also words for commanding angels. So, the stirring up or calling to attention another person's Personal Angel to their duty has been given to us. This is not outside our boundary. We have ability to do that.

The Bond Registry

Donna began seeing a book that looked like a Bond Registry. From the Bond Registry she was seeing pathways of light that go from the inside pages of registry. These pathways of light were the angel trails like a light beam. They were the paths of the Bond Registry Angels on assignment to deliver the bond to the person.

The angel bringing the bond is operating to bring what is written on the scroll to the person. When someone asks for the release of a bond, and that person goes to the court, follows the protocol, and requests the release of a particular bond, that bond gets registered. The Angels of the Bond Registry are then released to the realm of that person. If the person who originally asked for someone to request a bond for them is sensitive and perceiving, they will sense the recipients Personal Angel receive the angel of the registry and bring what the bond releases into their realm. It is a perceivable thing. Some of you have sensed that change. It is discernible, it is a spirit change and the result of angelic activity of both the Personal Angel and the Angel of the Bond Registry bringing the bond. It often will be written on a scroll. If you sense a delay, you can ask for the Personal Angel to be given backup to receive the Bond Registry Angel.

In some cases, Personal Angels are not practiced at receiving the Bond Registry Angel, so they may need instruction, or they may need angelic backup so that they can become experienced with receiving the registry angel.

In the case of a child, the Guardian Angel may need the help of the adult's angel to receive the Bond Registry Angel and learn this type of angelic duty.

Be sensitive to engage these angels and commission your angel(s) to cooperate with the Bond Registry angels for the fulfillment of what is in your scroll.

Chapter 14
Communication Pathways

I am going to share some deep things with you about the angelic realm—the hosts of Heaven. Communication pathways exist between angels on assignment and the those who are living on the earth.

Remember in scripture it is written that Jesus knew the thoughts and intent of men's hearts. He did that several times.[25] At one point, Jesus knew the people in the synagogue were planning to throw him off a cliff.[26] That is one example. In another passage, Jesus was dealing to the Pharisees and he was able to speak to them with wisdom because he knew the thought and intent of their heart.[27]

Jesus knew this information because an angel related it to Him. Remember, Jesus set aside his glory, and operated as a man, in a natural body while on the earth.

---

[25] Matthew 9:4, 12:25, 15:19, Luke 5:22, 6:8, 11:17
[26] Luke 4:29
[27] Matthew 12:25

So how did Jesus know the intent of the people? That information was translated by angels to him.

This is a work of the angelic. They do this only for purposes of the expansion of the Kingdom of God and from what is being written from the mouth of the Father. This angelic skill set is highly valuable to satanic occult forces and is often why angels are captured by realms of darkness.

Angels are meant and designed to operate with you, the believing saints. Notice I said the believing saints. Those who believe that angels can and do bring messages to them from the Father's Kingdom can interact with the angelic realm to receive these messages.

You have one way of thinking about what a message is, but a message is simply a communication. It is a point where information is shared.

The beings of Heaven can translate this to the spirits of humans who are sanctified and being continually redeemed by their seeking after Jesus and the Kingdom of God. The messages that angels bring are going to be especially important in the coming days. Pay attention to these messages. The forces of darkness are continually seeking ways to access this communication pathway to spy, hear or learn about the plans of Yahweh. The enemy wants to access these communications to frustrate or thwart the plan of Yahweh to bless the saints with His power and might, His goodness and kindness, and His redemptive purposes.

In the dark realms, spying is ancient practice. The forces of darkness have done this for a long, long time and have become adept at it. But greater understanding about the receipt of messages from the angelic hosts is coming to the Body of Christ, the Bride, so that she can operate in tandem with the Bridegroom.

While the Bridegroom may not be physically present in the earth realm now, He is present with His Bride in the spiritual places, where He has given access for the saints to join Him and to conduct business on His behalf.

The basic nugget you need to know is that angels are messengers, and they are now being released more and more frequently from Heaven with many things to share.

The messages of angels come for the present. They are not necessarily revealing the future, because as you are learning, *the future is forming*. The Father is counting on His sons and daughters to form the future with Him.

One day you might be doing something as simple as brushing your teeth and suddenly you know something new. You just have a knowing or you see a connection. Suddenly a dot connected to something you needed insight on and so, the information is dropped into your spirit. That was an angel bringing a message to you. The reason I am telling you this is because you are learning—you are being trained not to discount the messages of angels you have been receiving.

Some respected leaders in the body of Christ—especially in prophetic streams or in charismatic arenas—teach that the only one speaking to believers (or the only one allowed to speak to believers) is the Holy Spirit—that He is the only one bringing you these messages. Heaven respects that you respect the Holy Spirit, but Holy Spirit's work is also working with angels. Holy Spirit and angels are working together in this, and angelic messages are being delivered into the earth with more frequency and constancy. The body of believers who understand this process—who are seeking after and receiving Messenger Angels—are very few; but it is a global awakening and not limited to the United States alone.

For a long season, messages were brought in the form of dreams, but in more recent times, messages are coming more directly to our spirits as our spirit is gaining the freedom and liberty to receive. The teachings of the realms of Heaven, the Courts of Heaven and of spiritual senses involving the imagination is giving new insight for people to understand what their imagination is for. All these things are useful in what we call the communication pathway between humans and angelic beings.

For too long, the church has been distracted in the wrong direction. Much emphasis was placed on overcoming demons and demonic activity, to the exclusion of the angelic—who are an incredible gift to the Body of Christ. Angelic activity deserves our focus, because angels are more numerous than demons, are more powerful in every respect, and are far better equipped to deal with the demonic than humans are.

Wrong Alignments

Some humans in the earth have chosen realms of darkness and aligned themselves with lesser kingdoms to gain power in the present moment. Little do they know that what they surmise to be an increase in their power is sealing their eternity. In the world you are going to be aware of the activity that these people have aligned with and stirred up. Their activity opens portals that allow in dark spirits to afflict others.

I want to give you a real kindergarten understanding of how occult activity—rituals, sorcery, and witchcraft—works. It opens portals for dark spirits to come in. When those dark spirits come in, they do the dirty work of the person that is involved. This is what has happened over Portland, Oregon, in 2020, when rioting and looting took over parts of the city. A dark portal was opened that the angelic forces are working to close. A flood of demon spirits and other dark beings have come through that portal. What has happened is you are seeing the result of humanity being afflicted by the dark spirits. You can know that this was done intentionally and has been done in other places of the globe as well with equal intention.

But I need you to know that it has not gone unnoticed by Heaven, by Counsels of Heaven, by the angelic realm, and by the forces of Yahweh who will shortly put this down. Coronavirus and its manipulation about the earth was a similar activity. Let me give you a caution. This information is not for babies. It is meat not milk.

Knowing When Your Angel is Speaking

I have been instructed to walk lightly in this area of releasing this information, because it is going to be self-evident in the days to come. I have been suggesting to you that you can have conversations with angels, but you may not have understood that your angels are having conversations with you. That is the point that I want to illuminate and shed light on—how to know when your angel is speaking to you.

This knowing is going to come through your human spirit from the perception of your spiritual senses. Yes, your spiritual senses must be trained, disciplined, cleansed, and focused with the intent and desire of use and that use is sometimes resisted. It is resisted from the soul realm of a person *and* from outside dark activity *and* from doctrines of demons *and* from minds who have not fully aligned with the mind of the Lord, Jesus Christ.

Let me go back to something I said before. Remember I said this all has a purpose, and its purpose is for the expansion of the glory of the Kingdom in the earth realm. It is also expanding the territory of the Kingdom within people. Do not let this shock you, but it is expanding the Kingdom realm in heavenly places as well.

I remind you again, what you hear from me is often quite a hefty serving. It is not for the babies among you and you have many who are still babies. Therefore, courage and boldness were given because to eat this full meal, you must engage and receive the expansion that courage and boldness gives you. Courage and boldness have an activity that you have not fully understood. The oil of courage and boldness—remember it is from Heaven. It is Heaven's courage and boldness—not the soul realm's courage and boldness—and it has its own effect.

Some people heard what I said recently about courage and boldness and they stirred up their souls in courage and boldness. While this is not bad, it can be used for evil and it will wound people. When you use the information from your spirit man, in conjunction with the Holy Spirit, it has a completely different effect in expanding the kingdom of God.

Let us get back to the basics. The basic is that the angels of Yahweh have been released in greater numbers and with more frequency to bring the messages to his people. For many reasons such as protection, or to open new areas of understanding that humans are going to walk in. Some are bringing revelation how man can help man. Is not this just the goodness of God?

Chapter 15
Timed Devices

The weather was extremely windy and unsettled outside as we engaged Heaven on this Thursday. It seemed representative of the turmoil in the heavenlies. We were scheduled to meet with Ezekiel, who appeared with an hourglass in his hand. He had something he wanted to show us that was completely new, so he began to explain what the hourglass represented.

What he was holding was a timed explosive device. Satan has his version of this device, which is always meant for destruction, while the Father has his version, which is meant for destruction of the realms of darkness and expansion of the Kingdom of God. I will not go into all the details here, but I will provide you a little of the backstory.

The enemy has multiple planned disruptions over the next short while and, as the ecclesia, we need to be aware and be ready to release Heaven's weaponry for those events in advance.

Heaven said this:

"A planned disruption is known to the King and He desires the sons of His Kingdom to plant his own timed devices against forces of darkness and evil. This evil is not humankind being led astray or deceived. This is spiritual forces of darkness, principalities, and thrones set against the Kingdom of God in direct opposition against the Godhead who have led many astray and whom some worship. The evil is evil. This evil is worse than you think it is. It is deep darkness, deep evil, the destroyer along with the wicked variety of kingdoms—underwater, celestial, and other races. Their planned destruction has been timed as a disruption and it is now time for the sons of God to release the timing devices of Yahweh, of the Kingdom of Glory into the world.

In response to the enemy's planned disruption, the Father is releasing His own disruptors, His own timing devices. This timing device is a Kingdom Glory. This is a good thing. These timing devices are not for destruction. They are for the building up of the church and they are released as a response like the Father dares the enemy to use his disruptor because the Father then comes in with His overwhelming power of goodness and grace and causes moves of God, movements of the church, awakenings, even miracles, and things of that sort. We can count on this victory as we join the Lord in the air to release His timing devices—His own weapons of timed devices. We can do this with joy because it overwhelms darkness with light.

Angels are amassed and ready to release the Father's timed devices into the earth and the dark spiritual regions but are awaiting the participation of the saints. The ecclesia—two or more saints in agreement—must arise and release prayers in this regard.

Two saints can agree in prayer that timed devices would be planted with the activity of undercover angels (stealth mode) and that they would plant these in accordance with the maps of Heaven.

Where saints agree in prayer regarding this, the timed device of the Lord will be catapulted into dark regions. Dark regions are spiritual regions of darkness. These are spiritual places, not physical. Saints should request that angels will catapult these timed devices of the Lord into dark regions for their effect within the time of the season and era for which they were created.

I caution you. This is the work of the hands of angels. This weapon is not something that is available to you always. It is released only at certain times. Angels know when it is available, and they can let you know when it is available." Therefore, were informed this day by Ezekiel (the angel of our ministry).

"It is not unlimited. It is for a time. It is like a time within a time. So, there is a moment in time where angels know this weapon is released to be used by the saints. It is not inexhaustible. It has a supply and when the supply is over, it is over. The church and members of the Bride (the praying ecclesia—which is all saints, agreeing as touching this thing), are to release the angels to do their work in prayer by faith. This is a very specialized, highly regarded weapon of the Lord," Heaven said.

Of the two methods of release of the timed devices (1) Requesting their release into the earth by the hands of angels, or (2) Catapulting these devices into the realms of darkness; "Is one method preferred over the other?" we asked.

Heaven's response was, "Both are needed. Some will have more faith for one than the other. They will have more understanding of one than the other. Pray the prayer that you can pray with the most faith."

Heaven even gave us the prayer to pray:

Prayer for Timed Devices of the King of Glory for Distribution by the Hands of Angels Requested by the Saints in Prayer

Prayer 1:

In the name of the King, in agreement with scripture that says where two or more are gathered in the name of the King of glory, we choose now to co-labor with Heaven from earth regarding...

The Request of the Release of Timed Devices of the King of Glory to be Released into the Earth; *to be stealthily placed at the hands of angels of the heavenly host for this purpose; that Yahweh succeeds to victory and overwhelms the enemy due to the deployment of timed devices and their intended effect and results.*

We praise the Lord for his magnificent power, ability, and magnanimous virtue to overcome darkness, to turn evil to good, and to arrange His splendor upon the face of the earth.

We agree with this work and the release of the angels of the host of Heaven, and all associated angels engaged with this assignment to their work, commissioning them as the Sons of God in the name of Jesus Christ

Prayer 2:

To Deploy Timed Devices to the Realms of Darkness:

In the name of the King, in agreement with scripture that says where two or more are gathered in the name of the King of glory, we choose now to co-labor with Heaven from earth regarding...

The Request of the Release of Timed Devices to be Catapulted into Regions of Darkness. *We agree with the work of Yahweh, His love of the saints, His love for Jesus, His love for Himself, so as the three parts of the Trinity love themselves, we agree with this for the work of kindness, to the work of goodness, for the result of their agreement in cosmic geographies that affect planet earth. We come into agreement with His rule and reign in all spaces and release the angels of the host to their work regarding the release of the catapult containing timed devices of the Glory of God.*

We praise the Lord for his magnificent power, ability, and magnanimous virtue to overcome darkness, to turn evil to good, and to arrange His splendor upon the face of the earth.

We agree with this work and the release of the angels of the host of Heaven, and all associated angels engaged with this assignment to their work, commissioning them as the Sons of God in the name of Jesus Christ.

We must know that true prayer comes from Heaven. Some think that prayers are born in their soul realm. However, the will of the Father today is such that this prayer be released to as many who have faith. Timing is important as a key to victory in battle.

Some of you will think that I am speaking in political terms. I tell you plainly I am not. However, the results of these warfare tactics will affect all realms, including the political realm.

Resist the political spirit that is trying to give you means to think in terms of global politics at every turn. The world is about many more things than just the political spirit. However, many things are tied to it and are at stake in this hour. If you pray in tongues as you get ready to pray this prayer, this would be beneficial.

Chapter 16
Angelic Perceptions

Ezekiel had just appeared to us and was unusually brilliant in appearance. Once he appeared, he toned down his appearance as you would use a dimmer switch to turn down the brightness of a light fixture.

Ezekiel explained, "All angels are able to do this. We recognize that to speak with humanity we can do what you call 'dial down' the glory. We can do that with ease. Angels want to have relationship with you and so that they will do these things to enable the relationship."

He continued, "You have requested things on my behalf. The other side of that, the other end of that spectrum, is my work from the King of Glory on your behalf. It is a cycle of return that works together. Do not mistake that I am always at war or warring. That would be an incorrect understanding. Just like you are seeing me now relaxed in a relaxed state in the realms of Heaven."

Donna inquired, "So, I can meet with you in the realms of Heaven like this, and then in the next second, I can see you standing right there in my space? I still use the same spiritual eyes, but you are closer now. So, when you dial it up, I can know your presence here in my office, like you are standing here at the end of my desk. I can really tell that. Then, at some other point you step back into the realms of Heaven, but I can still see you like you are standing next to the Help Desk talking to me."

Ezekiel replied, "This is how angels come and go into your realm."

Donna noted, "You are a higher estate, but you in a higher estate can always manifest in a lower estate. The cloud of witnesses can do that too. That is interesting. You are giving me the understanding that this is twofold or doubled."

Ezekiel explained, "We are doubled because you can perceive when the realm of Heaven intersects or manifests in the natural. You can see it and sense it with different with spiritual senses. It is the same, but different."

"That is an interesting exercise of having your angel come near and then also having that angel step into the realms of Heaven and you step into Heaven to see the same being through Jesus, the door. Your spirit on the earth or in the realms of Heaven. You can engage both ways and you can do it quickly," Donna described.

As we continued to learn we marveled at the understandings Heaven was releasing to us.

Chapter 17
Court of Accounting

We had just concluded some bond registry work on behalf of one of our staff and were instructed in the Court of Reclamation to request an Amendment of Taxation against the enemy. This was a new understanding for us, and we were about to get an education. Here is some of the dialog from that encounter.

Donna (in the Court of Reclamation), "I request an amendment to this case because the verdict reveals we have caught a thief. The amendment is to place a tax on the enemy. I request as an amendment to this verdict in this case, that a tax be placed on the enemy for having engaged in this activity. I request this as a daughter of the Most High God, in the name of Jesus."

Ezekiel appeared because the staff member we were in court for was in his sphere, and he had knowledge of our court cases, our presentations in Heaven, and our questions about putting a tax on the enemy.

He began to explain this subject to us. When a saint or a son of God applies to Heaven for a tax on the enemy, this is putting a taxation on the enemy's trade. It creates a tax liability on the part of the enemy. A severe tax can be requested. There are some varying grades of the type of taxes that can be asked for. But the one called a Severe Tax on the enemy's trade is basically a deterrent to the enemy to cause him to stop a particular trade or to encourage him to shut down that trade route because we found out what he was doing from the Higher Kingdom.

As a believer, you have authority in the name of Jesus to place a tax on the enemy's evil trade. His trade is not illegal, it is simply evil. You can request of the Father and of His Kingdom to require of the enemy to pay a severe tax for that evil trade. Making this request highlights to the enemy that you know your authority in Jesus, that your Father's Kingdom is superior, and that his time messing around with you is done.

Ezekiel let us know that in days ahead, we would be learning more about this, but he was giving us the thumbnail sketch for right now. He continued, "You can ask of the Father and, out of his goodness, he can provide Taxing Angels who carry out the fulfillment of the tax on the enemy."

He explained the legality of how this amendment works. Sending your angel(s) to plunder the enemy's camp (that arena that he's not watching over) is one way of recovering what the enemy has stolen, but getting the amendment of taxation is done through the legal system of Heaven (like a court order) is amazingly effective. It is done through different channels than plundering. So, it does not engage your Personal Angels and does not take them off their assignment. Instead, it brings other angelic forces to the task when you request an amendment of taxation.

Whenever you are in court, particularly the Court of Reclamation, be sensitive to the counsel of the court. You may receive counsel to request an amendment of taxation against the enemy. If they counsel you in that manner, it is giving you the clearance to request that amendment. You will want to do that. Learning to wait on the counsel of the court is essential to know whether this is a measure that can be applied or not.

Heaven refers to it as an Amendment of Taxation. It places a tax on the trade that the enemy is using as he is engaged in evil trade. Evil trade is theft. Evil trade is character assassination. Evil trade is theft of proprietary information, theft of souls, theft of body parts, etc. You can see where these instances are.

It is hard to explain because we think in 3D, but it is the trade of the enemy, which is always evil, but it is not necessarily illegal trade. It is just evil trade because he trades no other way. There is nothing good in him, right?

What we leave with the Father is the accounting of this tax. That is Heaven's work, and there are many men and women in white linen attending to these accounting functions in Heaven and requiring the Taxing Angels to do their work. These Taxing Angels have authority to garnish what the enemy has stolen, gathered up, or accumulated.

As you are learning this, realize that you are processing this. Your spirit man is alive and understands; it is your soul that is still processing.

You may be directed to the Court of Accounting which, in vision form, seems to be the wing of a large building. The Court of Reclamation is in a wing of the Court of Accounting. They are all a part of Central Accounting. It is not a completely different building, but it is a definite separate wing with a lot of activity. Central Accounting also has a Help Desk as well where you can gain assistance or find out if you have a case, or cases, which you can request amendments for.

We approached the Help Desk and asked for assistance from the attendant. We explained that we were learning from Ezekiel about this court, and we wanted to know if we had any open cases that we could attach this amendment to retroactively.

With a flurry of questions, we asked, "Does it work for individuals? Does it work for businesses? How does it all work?"

An attending angel began to explain that where we were was known as Central Accounting. If you are a business or ministry that has received your Declaration of Trade, you can obtain this information in the Financial Department. The angel explained that when-ever someone does work of an accounting nature in the Business Complex, it is recorded in Central Accounting. It is flowing to them in the background. You can discover the answer about cases that need an amendment in the Financial Department of the Business Complex or at the Help Desk of Central Accounting. Just ask the attendant (in either locale) to show you if there are any accounting irregularities, outstanding accounting entries, or taxation of the enemy that you might pursue from a business/ministry, or trade orientation. That attendant will be able to help you.

If you are doing this for families, individuals, nations, communities, and entities that are not businesses or ministries you can ask at the Help Desk of Central Accounting.

We explained that we were just in the Court of Reclamation and were told to ask for an Amendment of Taxation about an item. Central Accounting had a record of that request.

Our question was, "Is there any taxation that we might request to be place on the enemy retroactively or otherwise?" (Because we had just found out about this.)

The angel's response was that all things are possible. The angel explained that there is a statute of limitations of a sort. If you are going too far back to try to tax the enemy, you may not be permitted to do so. When asking why a statute of limitations might be in place, the angel simply said "I cannot tell you that. Some things are not yet opened to all."

If we feel led to pursue a retroactive taxation on the enemy, we can come to Central Accounting and ask at the Help Desk if we are able to bring that case. If we are, we will be ushered into the Court of Accounting to bring the case for taxation against the enemy.

The angel explained that we would have to get used to the nuances of this court and its protocols, which means, among other things, that we would be learning to wait on the counsel of these particular courts.

In the Court of Reclamation, you must wait for the attendants to tell you what you can reclaim. You cannot simply make a blanket reclamation request. It is the same when pursuing a retroactive court case for taxation against the enemy.

Asking the angel for an easy example to walk us through the process, she began looking in folders. She retrieved a recent situation with someone who we had an unpleasant experience with, resulting in some slander and hardship being brought to the ministry by the work of evil. She recommended that we use that case as an example.

Donna began, "Father, I ask permission to enter the Court of Accounting on behalf of LifeSpring International Ministries, in the name of Jesus. I have been told by the Help Desk that I have access to a retroactive case of taxation against the enemy regarding a client of LifeSpring. We are requesting a tax be placed against the enemy for rendering us an undue hardship and slander. Our plea is that we engaged in righteous trade in good faith with this client and our testimony is that we have forgiven this client. We continue to forgive her, bless her, and release her. We are looking for a verdict of a retroactive taxation against Satan and his Kingdom regarding this. We ask this in Jesus' name."

Having made our plea, several accounting angels appeared and began looking on databases and jotting down notes. They were verifying our request.

Once they verified the request, they took the paperwork to the bench and we awaited the verdict.

The verdict was then announced by the court, "The verdict is Taxation on Trade on Evil Realms Through Use of a Person's Voice for Evil Means." Asked if that was our request, we concurred. "We do request this in the name of Jesus."

The court continued, "So, ruled on our behalf against the enemy. Marked today: 11/6/2020.

With that, we exited after thanking the court, the angel assisting us and Ezekiel our ministry angel for his tutelage. Of course, we also thanked the Father.

Now, Heaven would handle the details. Taxing Angels would be released to garnish from the enemy according to the verdicts of the court.

You may have cases that you want to access Central Accounting about. The more you understand your authority, the more you understand that you do not have to let the enemy run roughshod over you. Instead, you know who you are, and who you belong to, and you understand that Heaven has solutions. This taxation of the enemy is simply another in the myriad of solutions Heaven is unveiling to the saints.

Within a few days of our first engagement with the Accounting Complex, we were going to receive more insight on this fascinating place. Most of us do not usually think of accounting as fascinating, but Heaven has a way of making it feel like that!

We were taken to the Accounting Complex, where a great number of angels were considerably busy. They seemed quite serious about their work. In an overview, Ezekiel began to share some of the various courts in this complex. We saw a door that said Court of Tabulations, one that said Court of Subtractions and another that said Court of Storehouse.

One had the sense of old-fashioned devices such as abacuses, adding machines, and cash registers here, but it was also very efficient. Most of the workers here were angels. Only a few men in white linen could be seen, unlike what you might see in other courts.

All Things are Counted

Mitchell, a man in white linen who was accompanying us, explained that we think of accounting in terms of figures, numbers, and currency amounts. That is true in the Court of Accounting too, *but* (and you will need to expand your thinking right now) it is also about the accounting of words, letters (like alphabet letters), and hopes and dreams. It is a counting of books. It is the counting of warfare. Heaven said,

"All things have an accounting and are counted."

Times, seasons, calendars, minutes, nations, people groups, individuals, large and small gatherings of people—all are being precisely counted and recorded. The sense of the quantity of things counted in Heaven is hard to fathom. Even minute things are accounted for. We know from scripture that the hairs of our head are counted.[28] We may have thought that to be allegorical, but Heaven is showing us differently.

Court of Proving

Another way to look at the Court of Accounting is the Court of Proving.[29] This court proves out the Word of

---

[28] Luke 12:7
[29] Court of Proving is not a separate court, it is simply another applicable name for the Court of Accounting due to the nature of accounting.

God. It is the accounting of the Word of God in you and in your realm, in your children, and in His children. In those awakened, not awakened, and partially awakened.

There is just so much to take in, that it is a little overwhelming. Every molecule, every grain of sand, every speck of DNA, every hair is numbered and recorded in the Court of Accounting. That is why Heaven referred to it as a thumbnail sketch in our previous encounter.

Heaven continued,

Nothing created exists that has not been counted.

And all things that have not been, or that have not yet been created, have been counted as well.

Court of Accounting of the Works of Darkness

A wing of this complex is present that keeps track of darkness. It counts the wages of sin. It counts the iniquity of the nations. It counts the deceiver's lies. It counts the stolen ideas and the stolen glory like in idolatry. This is what Daniel saw into and what John saw into and recorded in Revelation. John entered the Court of the Accounting of the Works of Darkness.

We noticed that there are Sentry Angels[30] at this hallway. This is a very protected wing. The angels that come and go from this area look different from the those in the other areas. They are much more warrior-like, and in fact they carry arms.

Court of the Accounting of the Words of the Saints.

The Court of the Accounting of the Words of the Saints was a more enjoyable wing to discover. This department keeps track of the words spoken in agreement with the King, in His behalf and on His Royal Decree. This accounting wing also records the thoughts and intents of every heart that is in alignment with the will of God—but not *just* the will of God. It also includes the exact perfection of his sovereignty.

We were told that this is a room from everlasting to everlasting, as is most of Heaven. We were asked, "Do you feel the palpable vibration of the word, even though you don't hear any words being spoken?"

Donna described what she was sensing, "Yes. It feels like a force of agreement. It is profoundly powerful. It is almost like an earthquake and the voice of many waters, like what you would think the power of a tsunami would hold." Some of what we call words are the intent of the heart and the intent of the will that align with the

---

[30] Sentry Angels stand guard over specific places.

sovereignty of the King. They have not yet even been born to the verbal in the physical realm, but are, in essence, awaiting their birth.

Heaven said, "You can tell the family of God that their prayer language is counted here as well, as well as all prophecy—that is, true prophecy.

All thoughts and intents of the heart that are of faith and a purity of righteousness in belief of Yahweh's power and position—these are all accounted here.

Tell the family of God, open your mouth, open your mouth, open your mouth, and agree with God."

Many still do not know understand the power of the spoken word. Instruct the Bride to release this power through:

- the power of the spoken scripture—verbally pray aloud scripture,
- the verbal release of speaking in tongues,
- the verbal release of the blessing of Yahweh to order all things according to God's sovereignty

Many are watching for The Bride to begin operating in this verbal authority. Many men and women in white linen are assigned to watch for this. Many angels are assigned to record these things because these verbal releases fill up the heart of God. They fill up His pleasure and delight in His creation. They fill up His purpose and many intangible things. They are all accounted here in the Accounting Complex of Heaven.

Heaven challenged us to try to count every leaf that fell in one day in the autumn all over the planet. We could not even do that in just a portion of our yard.

Heaven reminds us:

> *Nothing goes unnoticed.*

Heaven said, "Remind the family of God that nothing goes unnoticed."

As we were marveling at the immensity of Heaven's accounting processes, Ezekiel reminded us that there is still more we have not seen. He exclaimed, "I haven't even shown you the accounting of the Court of Praise!"

Balancing

One of the functions of the accounting that takes place in Heaven is also the balancing. There are many balances in Heaven. Things are being weighed and viewed, and consideration is given to how the item balances with the King of Glory and His Kingdom will. These things are related to God's sovereignty and that He has given himself to the enjoyment of humanity and what He has created.

Heaven explained, "When I say to you, 'balances and things being balanced', most of Western civilization has a negative connotation of this thought—like a shortfall being calculated. Heaven desires you to have a new thinking in place of that. Heaven wants you to understand that Yahweh is delighted in what the balance has been, what the balance is, and what the balance will come to. It is all three tenses—what has been, what is, and what it will be—and the result is always perfection."

It was born from the Father's own perfection, therefore the view of balances and weights and things being considered and noted whether they are in balance can always proceed through hope because...

Hope always wins and hope will lead you to the viewpoint of victory.

That's what I'm going to leave you with today—the viewpoint of victory that hope will give you because the hope of Heaven and Heaven's hope within His children will bring forth the intended sovereign glory.

Chapter 18
Insights

We had been having difficulty with our Internet connections this particular day, but were not deterred in engaging Heaven. We asked Ezekiel if he wanted to discuss anything else in this visit, and he began, "You have heard it said angels are powerful and mighty and we are, yet, we don't reveal this power to you as much as we reveal our power and might to the enemies of your soul, and especially to Satan, as a defeated foe. We welcome your belief in our given power and might and your faith in our ability," Heaven explained.

The Might of Angels

Your faith makes us stronger, but it effactually makes our relationship stronger as well. Your faith in our ability to accomplish our assignments on your behalf is helpful and it is okay for you to believe more in our power, for we are powerful and mighty.

We often do not reveal ourselves to you in this way, but let me tell you, the enemy knows when we arrive on the scene. Heaven impressed us to share with you—that you may see your angel, or the angel of your business, but the angel is presenting himself to you in a certain way. It is the same as how you present yourselves differently at work than you do to your close friends. Remember this.

Ezekiel had some requests for us that day, but one of the requests was unusual. He requested a Military Encampment.

When asked to explain this to us, he obliged. As his ranks grow, and as our ministry grows, he gets backup—meaning, more angels to assist him. He needs a place for these angels to gather, and this is a spiritual place called his military encampment. He wanted us to know that this would be his second encampment. He explained that when backup comes, this encampment is where those angels get provisions, receive their orders, and have communication.

He went on to explain that he had received recognition from the Father for good work done and he always appreciates when he sees our ministry grow because he gets expanded territory as well. This makes him happy. It also keeps him busy.

This growth of our ministry is one of the reasons for the new military encampment. Ezekiel also wanted us to note that he takes his duty seriously. At that point, we requested of the Father the Military Encampment Ezekiel needed. We also made a point to commend him to the Father for a job well done. We recommend you do the same periodically for your angel(s).

Ezekiel was pleased and honored that he received the expansion, as it also included an expansion of his duties his oversight. He explained that angels enjoy increase, and they enjoy increasing in rank, level, and expansion. The busier they are, the larger their duty within their realm. To have oversight for these things is pleasurable to angels because they have assignments from the Father that they are eager to accomplish. The worst thing for an angel is to have an assignment, but always be stymied by their human counterparts—whether through human ignorance, sin, or the human being distracted to pursue wrong things. He explained that his fellow angels recognize his activity, his duty, and his expanded oversight due to how we are engaging him. He pointed out that angels do not get jealous, but they do recognize when they are being utilized and when the relationship with their human is being built.

Working with our angels was a definite lesson that day. The angels of God from the supernatural realm will make a supernatural event out of any event. They will position supernatural things that we could not do in our dimension via our working with our angel. Some things cannot happen because we are limited. We are only operating from the natural, but when we collaborate with the angels, they operate from the higher dimension of the supernatural and will enact things that manifest in the natural that look impossible.

Provisioning

As we continued, we asked for clarity on a subject. We asked Ezekiel to help define the provisioning aspect of our relationship with the Father.

Ezekiel explained that while he often comes and requests particular things that we might request of the Father on his behalf, Heaven continually provisions and re-provisions him as an angel assigned to the ranks. This is true for every angel.

He continued, "Our increase comes from your commendation, but it also comes when you request special things for us. Please understand this does not mean that we always need you to ask on our behalf, because the heavenly Father has well provisioned us for our tasks and what we need. However, your spoken requests in our behalf cause the Father to act. Sometimes your suggestion on when to do a thing or what to do is necessary. For instance, when you command us to come and put a demon in chains, or when you command us to assist you in the unseen with a particular thing. We are always interested to do that because this includes us in what you are perceiving from the Spirit of the Lord. It completes a circuit of agreement, because we are always in agreement with what the Father is saying.

For this reason, you may not sense your angel needing very much provisioning today, even though they may have been involved in all sorts of activity. Ezekiel said, "Where Heaven sees a deficit, Heaven fills the deficit for the angelic ranks."

He says, "Don't get me wrong. If you stopped what you have been learning to do, we would notice lack of engagement on our behalf and may be somewhat disappointed. We do have emotions about these things, but our emotions are different than emotions from the humanity on God's earth. Our emotions are much more in line with the activity of Heaven and its realms. However, we do, we do experience emotion."

He says, "Remember, I am using language you can understand, but we are often aggrieved or rubbed the wrong way by humanity's actions. This has made angels among us go astray and has caused rupture within ranks. However, our purpose in assisting you is always aided by your assisting us—and this mutual co-laboring is what we all hope to do to accomplish the work of the Kingdom. has increased His glory and the manifestation of His name, and this is only going to increase in days ahead. Get ready. This co-laboring is only going to increase in coming days. There are some things in the past that will remain in the past, but there are many things in the future that are brand new. The past is providing a launching point for the new."

"Now," he says, "I am going to ask you for a new weapon, because I want you to know that I have this weapon. It is an intelligent rifle." He says, "You might call it a smart gun. It is laser equipped for realms of darkness and assists us in plundering, freeing, taking back territory that has been stolen by darkness, and ensuring the new territory stays regained." He says, "You can just take this at face value. Some things you do not need to wrap your mind around because there's really no equation that it can cross to in your understanding."

Donna said to me, "Ron, Ezekiel is fully aware of what he needs to do, but he enjoys it when you commission him to go on patrol."

Ezekiel says, "Do you not find it interesting that today we were able to tell you that there was a breach into the realm so that communications would be destroyed, and how it manifested in your realm was an internet issue—a complete mess." Ezekiel also explained that the rash of 'no show' appointments, issues with time zones and people having problems connecting for their sessions just seemed like a flurry of aggravations; however, as he explained, they were all connected. Things that happen in the spiritual realm do manifest in the earthly realm.

The purpose of the requests on behalf of our angel is that it creates a co-laboring with Heaven on our part. If we simply assumed that all provision would be made automatically by Heaven, we might miss valuable opportunities to engage with Heaven and co-labor with those who co-labor with us.

Ezekiel on Sending Representatives

Because we have talked about Ezekiel so openly with so many people, we have found that some people outside of our formal organizational hierarchy take the liberty of trying to connect with him. They are asking for Ezekiel, or trying to put Ezekiel to work, so we asked him about this.

Ezekiel said," I do cover a great many things. Your people need to know that often when they call for me, I do not come to them. I send someone in my ranks. I have many who answer to me. Remember the Centurion and Jesus,[31] as they discussed what faith will accomplish. The Centurion explained that when he spoke to a servant to come, the servant came and if he spoke to a servant to go, the servant went. On the same basis, Jesus spoke the word and the healing came. Faith was a servant and faith fulfilled the assignment faith was given. Jesus was utilizing the armies of Heaven. One way you can understand this is to look at your earthly armies and recall that when you have need of the general, you will not often get the general himself, but his representative who carries the authority that the general has delegated to him. So, you need to share with your people that I have a strict assignment. I am aware of my realms of authority, but I am also aware of those who answer to my authority within angelic ranks. Often, I will send

---

[31] Matthew 8:5-13

them on assignment to those who are calling me near, but I am not the one coming."

Ezekiel continued, "They need to understand the ranks of angels. They need not to think of angels as myths or fairytales. They need to think and move as maturing saints from their spirit. Their spirit will perceive differently."

"You have a few who are still operating immaturely," he explained, "however, they are moving in the realms of Heaven. I do not regret this, but I am letting you know that some are sharing inconsistencies with one another behind the scenes when they are not with you. They are saying things like, 'I saw Ezekiel' and 'Ezekiel told me this', or 'Ezekiel went here for me'." Ezekiel explained saying, "This is simply incorrect. I am coming to set the record straight so you can share, directly from Ezekiel, that that I send myself where I need to go based on my assignments. I send representatives from my ranks where they are needed and when they are needed. Thinking that I am the one showing up in their space is proof of immaturity. That is just not how it works."

Completing his discourse, Ezekiel said, "I need them to understand. I do not mind them being immature. Do you see that from the realms of Heaven, we understand your growth pattern and we understand your maturing and the levels you go through in this, but there is a point where this must be plainly stated, so I came to tell you this today."

We have noticed that Heaven will be quite blunt at times. When something needs to be said plainly, it will be. That is just how Heaven does things.

The Supercharging Effect

When angels arrive on a scene, their presence creates a supercharging of what is transpiring. This supercharging effect angels bring is one you will want to explore. When angels are invited into a situation, they essentially supercharge the person with what has been lacking in the persons' life. This is particularly evident when the person has been at a severe deficit in an arena of their life and they have felt as if they were out of options.

This supercharging effect, Heaven reminded us, is what we heard one of our attendees on a Tuesday night session share about the young lady who asked her angel to come near and she could feel an immediate difference within her. The angel did nothing except come close to the young woman and the energy (the faith) the attendee carried by believing that if the young woman asked, her angel would come near precipitated the appearance of her angel. By coming close, the love the angel carried overrode any sense of fear that was prevalent in the young woman.

So, it is with the supercharging effect—if someone is dominated by chaos or confusion, when their angel is called near, they bring peace intended to overtake any confusion. A person can request (for themselves or for another person) that an angel bring what that person lacks for themselves. The request is made of the Father, but the angel is the courier to deliver the request.

Many times, we have not understood or utilized this powerful dynamic and have gone lacking as a result. Think about when the early church lacked boldness or wanted an increase of boldness. It was not so much that Holy Spirit was released to bring the boldness—the angels became the couriers of the release of boldness.

For Jesus, Holy Spirit was not indwelling Him at the time of His ministry upon the earth because at that point in time Holy Spirit was in Heaven. The delivery system for the messages he received were the angelic hosts assigned to Him for that purpose. The voice He heard was angels. They may have been speaking what the Father had them relay to Him, but He had laid down his divinity at that point. He was not working from divinity but from humanity. When the Father spoke, He spoke audibly to Jesus at times, and at other times through angels.

The Resonance of Angels

The resonance of angels (a result of their frequency) is designed to bring peace to your human body. Often you read of groups of people hearing a chorus of angels as they all worship together. It is not just angels they are hearing. They are also hearing choirs of Heaven made up of men and women in white linen. Their sound is quite spectacular.

Where you have dissonance in your body, invite your angel to bring it into harmony with Heaven. Many have worked with frequencies and have come up with all kinds of solutions, but the simplest solution is to allow your angel—who is already attuned to the frequencies of Heaven—to release the frequencies of Heaven in you.

Offensive & Defensive Stances

We had noticed a slight downturn in connections with people for sessions, products, and the like. We asked for some insights about it and Ezekiel assisted us.

He explained, "You need to remember the battle is both offensive and defensive. So, charge me and my ranks with both offensive and defensive actions."

Here is what that looks like. His ranks can dissuade those not assigned by the commander (Jesus, the King) to locate the ministry's trade, meaning our services. Ezekiel and his ranks know who can and who will be best served by our trade with them. He knows those who will be a distraction. A distraction is a type of theft. They know the difference between those who will be a distraction and those who will be served. Ezekiel wants to be charged that the ministry produces fruit for the kingdom of God.

Ezekiel continued, "Charge me to harvest the fruit for you and to weed out those not able to gain fruit from you.

Other ministries exist and are assigned certain clients—those clients should not come to you. You want to charge me to gather those whom you are to serve and those who will become fruit for this ministry because of our trade. You do not want to waste your time—or theirs. It is okay to know that not all will be benefited by your trade because they need another expression of a trade. However, some clients are meant for you and will be fruit that remains.

Charge me with gathering the people who are ordained to work with your ministry. Some will not be served by your program and they will not be your fruit, because fruit for this ministry is fruit for the kingdom."

Immediately we issued the following charge to him,

"In the name of Jesus, we charge you Ezekiel, your commanders, and your ranks with gathering to LifeSpring International Ministries those clients for the business sessions, the personal sessions, the book purchases and the membership purchases that will bring fruit to this ministry—a great harvest that will be fruit to the King and to the Kingdom. We charge you to do this offensively and defensively. We ask you to prevent from locating our trade those who would be a distraction as clients and those who would not bear fruit for this ministry. We ask you to dissuade them, as they are not assigned by the Father to engage with our ministry. We charge you to this in Jesus' name."

We noted a Scribing Angel was present who was writing all that down and we felt we had learned another key to the successful growth of the ministry. Whenever you see prayers and charges like the prayer in italics thus far, simply tailor it to your situation—whether personal, ministry, or business.

More About Plundering

We asked, "Is there further commissioning concerning the plunder of the enemy's camp?"

Ezekiel explained, "With this charge (the one above in italics) to gather and dissuade is an implied association to plunder. Where angels need to plunder, they will plunder.

*Angels are always willing to hear the charge
to plunder the enemy's camp.*

The righteousness of the Father's kingdom also includes those treasures that have been left behind by others who did not pick them up and gather them into their storehouses. They did not loose their angels to plunder and bring in the spoils. A lot has been left on the battlefield, and angels cannot touch it until believers' request that the angels go and get that which was left behind by other ministries or other individuals. It is fruit left on the battlefield and it belongs to King Jesus."

With that, we gave him a charge:

"We charge you, Ezekiel, in Jesus' name, to go collect the spoils of battle and bring them into the storehouse of the ministry."

He explained, "A lot of your spoils involves readers and/or book purchasers. Their hearts are hungry, but their hunger for the truth and the righteousness has not been filled yet."

Again, with that in mind we charged Ezekiel:

"We charge you to bring those hungry for what we trade in, into the storehouse in the name of Jesus."

Ezekiel continued, "It is like where you see a battle between the victorious armies of the Lord and the enemy. After the battlefield is exited, treasure is left on the battlefield that the angels have not been loosed to gather yet."

He encouraged us and we encourage you to join with us and say, *"Gather! Yes, plunder and gather!"*

Chapter 19
Conclusion

You can never return to the same size container you were in prior to reading this book. You may have been intrigued, challenged, strengthened, encouraged, or any number of other things as you read it and you may even be struggling to reconcile what you have read in these pages with what you have been taught in the church or with your own worldview. Understand that Heaven is simply reaching out to you, to bring you into fuller realms of understanding and closeness with the Father.

Francois Du Toit in his translation of Hebrews 1:14 says this, "What role do the celestial messengers play in God's strategy? They are all employed by God in the prophetic-apostolic ministry of the Spirit to help administer the inheritance of salvation that belongs to mankind."[32]

---

[32] The Mirror Translation (Du Toit)

That sums up what we have shared in this book rather well. It is our prayer that you receive the impartation of life that is resident in this book, and that you begin to engage with your Personal Angels on a daily basis, that you receive the Messenger Angels that are sent to you, and that you step into entirely new levels of faith in your walk with the Father.

Let revelation continue to have impact in your life. Be changed and become a vessel of change on an entirely new level. May you be blessed with richer and fuller understandings of the goodness of the Father in your life.

Appendix A

Accessing the Realms of Heaven

One tremendous privilege that we share during this time in history is the ability to access the realms of Heaven with ease.[33] Many of us were taught that Heaven is only for after we die. Heaven *is* a final destination on our journey, but can also be a vital part of that journey.

What I am about to share is crucial in order to progress within the various Courts of Heaven. We can access the Mercy Court (see the next chapter) while firmly planted here on the earth, but to maximize our endeavors in the Courts of Heaven, we need to learn how to operate FROM Heaven.

When teaching on accessing the realms of Heaven, I often point out some simple facts. If you were to tell me

---

[33] From *Engaging the Courts of Heaven* by Dr. Ron M. Horner Copyright ©2018 All Rights Reserved

you were a citizen of a particular town, but you could tell me little about the town from your personal experience, I would have a tendency to doubt the authenticity of your citizenship. I am a citizen of a small town in central North Carolina. I am familiar with the location of the city hall, police station, hospital, local county courthouse, Sheriff's Department and much more. I know where many sporting events will be held. I know where the parks are. I know many of the stores and restaurants. I am familiar with this small town. Yet, if I were to ask the average believer what they can describe of Heaven from personal experience, the answer would likely be, "Nothing". They have no personal experience of Heaven that they can relate to me. It does not have to be like that.

In Matthew 3, Jesus informed us that the Kingdom of Heaven was at hand. We could say, "the Kingdom of Heaven is as close as your hand." Hold your hand up in front of your nose as close as you can. Do not touch your nose. Heaven is closer to you than that. It is not far, far away, up in the sky. It is not "over yonder" as some old hymns describe. It is a very present reality separated from us by a very thin membrane—and we can access it by faith. It is quite simple.

When Jesus was baptized in the River Jordan, as he came up out of the water, IMMEDIATELY the Heavens were opened. He both saw (a dove) and heard (a voice coming from Heaven). This one act of Jesus restored our ability to access Heaven. We can experience open Heavens over our lives. We do not have to wait. We can live conscious of the realm of Heaven and live out of that reality!

Everything we do as believers we must do by faith. Accessing the realms of Heaven is done the same way. Prophetic acts can create realities for us, and it is the same with this. You can visualize stepping from one room into another easily. It is like stepping from one place to another. To learn to access the realms of Heaven, you will follow the same pattern.

Stand up from where you are now and prepare to work with me. You can experience the realms of Heaven right now! You do not have to wait until you are dressed up in a long box at the local funeral home or filling an urn. You can experience Heaven while you are alive! Remember, we enter the Kingdom as a child.

How to Access Heaven

Quiet yourself down. Turn off distracting background noises, if possible. Prepare to relax and focus. Now, say this with me:

Father, I would like to access the realms of Heaven today, so right now, by faith, I take a step into the realms of Heaven.

As you say that, close your eyes and take a step forward. As you step forward, imagine you are going from one place to another in a single step. Once you have done so, pay attention to what you see and hear. You may see very bright lights, you may see a river, a pastoral scene, a garden—any number of things. Right now, you are experiencing a taste of Heaven. You will notice the peace that pervades the atmosphere of Heaven. You might notice the air seems electric with life. The testimonies I have heard are always amazing and beautiful to hear.

Now spend a few minutes in this place. Remember, Jesus said that to enter the Kingdom, you must come as a little child. I often coach people to imagine yourself as an 8-year-old seeing what you are seeing. What would an 8-year-old do? He or she would be inquisitive and ask, "What is this? What does that do? Where does that go? Can I go here?" If a child saw a river or a lake, what would that child want to do? Most would want to jump into the water.

The variety is infinite. The colors are amazing! The sounds are so beautiful. You can learn to do this on a regular basis. When you access the realms of Heaven, you are home. You were made to experience the beauty that is Heaven.

The reason it is important to learn to access the realms of Heaven is that much of what we do in the Courts of Heaven needs to be done FROM Heaven. We need to learn to engage Heaven and work from it.

Seeing versus Knowing

Many people tell me they cannot "see" visually in the spirit. Often, they are discounting the ability they do have. They may be discounting their "knower." Every believer has a "knower" at work within them. This "knower," who is Holy Spirit at work within you, helps you perceive things. Whether something is good or evil, He works to guide you more than you may have realized.

Most navy submarines have a device known as sonar. Sonar gives a submarine "eyes" to see what is in their vicinity. They can detect what the object is by the ping emitted by the sonar. They can determine the distance to the object and whether it is another submarine. They can even identify what class of submarine it might be. Sonar is invaluable in this setting where a video camera would be rather useless underwater.

The military has a similar device for above ground situations known as radar. It functions in much the same way as the sonar. If a pilot were flying through thick cloud cover, he would need to know what is in his path. Radar becomes his eyes.

Some people function visually. They often see what amounts to pictures or video images when they "see" in the spirit. They may see more detail. Yet one operating by his or her "knower" (their spiritual radar or sonar) can be just as effective as a seer. If you operate more like sonar or radar, do not discount what you "see" in that manner. It is how I function, and I have been doing this type of work for many years.

I can often detect where an angel is in the room (or if it is one of the men or women in white linen and not an angel). I can often detect how many are present and whether they have something they are to give to someone. I can detect any number of things and even though it is not "visual" it is still a form of "seeing." It will set your mind at ease when you understand that operating by your "knower" is just as valid as any other type of vision. It will help you to realize you have been seeing much more than you know and you may know much more than some who only see.

Factors Hindering Seeing or Hearing

When someone tells me they have trouble seeing or hearing in the realm of the spirit, I have found a common cause for much of the problem. Most of us have some measure of Freemasonry in our background. As part of the oaths and ceremonies of Freemasonry, one makes a covenant with their eyes to not be able to see spiritually. They symbolize this with the act of putting on the hoodwink (or blindfold) in the early initiation ceremonies. They are making a covenant to be spiritually blind. If they did not make this kind of covenant in the early stages of Freemasonry, they would be able to see the darkness they are getting themselves involved in.

The person needs to get the false verdicts empowering Freemasonry overturned in their lives. I recommend my book, *Overcoming the False Verdicts of Freemasonry*. I have found a correlation between Freemasonry and the inability to see or hear spiritually about 90% of the time.

The second situation I have found is the person who has made a covenant with their eyes not to see. Usually this is the result of having been frightened earlier in their life when they saw something spiritually. This can happen particularly with a small child who may see something in a dream or vision, and it frightens them so much that they shut down the seeing or hearing.

The resolution for this is to become willing to step back into the scene that frightened them, but this time, invite Jesus to be with them in the situation. When he shows up, the fear seems to dissipate. I ask them to repent for shutting down the spiritual vision and/or hearing part of their life and have them ask Jesus to reopen their seeing or hearing.

The last situation we have recently discovered is that someone has gotten a false title, lien, note, or lease agreement that blocks the person's ability to see in the spirit, or somehow the enemy has placed a tarpaulin (tarp[34]) over them to block seeing and hearing.

---

[34] A large sheet placed to cover or protect objects. In the natural, they are usually made of canvas or plastic.

We step into the Court of Titles & Deeds and request that every false title of ownership or false note over our spiritual sight or hearing be dissolved, and the ownership of the Lord Jehovah be established over our spiritual eyes and ears.

If it involves a lien against our ability to see or hear, we request that it be marked satisfied by the blood of Jesus. We forgive the person or persons involved in making the false claim of ownership, we bless them, and we release them.

If a lease agreement is involved, we also ask that the false lease agreement be cancelled, and a righteous ownership claim be established between the person and the Lord Jehovah.

We also request any tarpaulins (tarps) over their eyes and life be immediately removed. We have seen immediate results when doing this as people's spiritual eyes are suddenly opened as well as their spiritual ears.[35]

---

[35] From *Engaging the Courts of Heaven* by Dr. Ron M. Horner Copyright ©2018 All Rights Reserved

Learning to Live Spirit First

A challenge with how we were taught about the Christian life is that everything was put off until sometime in the future. Then, we read the letters of Paul and we experienced a disconnect. Heaven, to us, was a destination, not a resource. We knew nothing about learning to live from our spirits. We only knew what we had been doing all our lives, since birth, and that is to live to satisfy our soul or our flesh. We sorely need to learn an alternative way of living.

Exchanging Your Way of Living

Paul recorded these words in his letter to the Romans:

Those who are motivated by the flesh only pursue what benefits themselves. But those who live by the impulses of the Holy Spirit are motivated to pursue spiritual realities. Romans 8:5

We must learn to live spirit first! We must exchange our way of living. We must learn to live from our spirit. We need to understand the hierarchy within us:

- We are a spirit
- We possess a soul
- We live in body

Each component has a specific purpose in our lives. Our spirit is the interface with the supernatural realm. It is designed for interfacing with Heaven & the Kingdom realm. Your spirit has been in existence in your body since your conception. Your soul has a different purpose. It communicates to your intellect and your physical body what your spirit has obtained from Heaven. It is the interface with your body. Your body houses the two components and will follow the dictates of whichever component is dominating,

Most of us have never been taught about having our spirit dominate. Rather, we have merely assumed that our soul being dominant was the required mode of operation.

Our soul always wants to be in charge. Our soul is susceptible to carnal or fleshly desires, lusts, and behaviors. It will, at times, resist our spirit and body. It must be made to submit to your spirit by an act of your will.

Your will is a means of instructing either component (spirit, soul, or body) what to do. Your soul has a will and so does your spirit. You choose who dominates!

Your body, on the other hand, has appetites that will control you in subjection to your soul. They become partners in crime—remember that second piece of chocolate cake it wanted? Your body will try, along with your soul, to dictate your behavior. It will likely resist the spirit's domination of your life. However, it will obey your spirit's domination if instructed, and your body can aid your spirit if trained to do so.

The typical expression that operates in most peoples' lives is that their soul is first, body second, and their spirit is somewhere in the distance in last place.

In some people, especially those very conscious of their physical fitness or physical appearance, there is a different line up. Their body is their priority, the soul second, and again their spirit is the lowest priority.

Heaven's desire for us is vastly different. Heaven desires that we live spirit first, soul second, and body third. Since we are spiritual beings, this is the optimal arrangement. For most of us, our spirit was not activated in our life in any measure until we became born again.

If, after our salvation experience, we began to pursue our relationship with the Father, then we became much more aware of our spirit and learning to live more spirit conscious. The apostle Paul wrote in his various epistles about living in the spirit or walking in the spirit. Because we are spiritual beings, our spirits cry out for a deepening of relationship with the Father. Your spirit longs for it and will try to steer you in that direction.

Our soul has certain characteristics that explain its behavior in our life. This is the briefest of lists, but I think you will get the idea. Our soul is selfish. It wants what it wants when it wants it. It can be very pouty. It can act like a small child. It is offendable and often even looks for opportunities to be offended. Our soul is also rude.

Our body has a different set of characteristics. It is inconsiderate, demanding, lazy, and self-serving. It does not want to get out of bed in the morning, for many people. In others, it wants to be fed things that are not beneficial.

However, characteristics of our spirit are hugely different. If we live out of our spirit, we will find that we are loving and prone to be gentle. We desire peace. We are considerate. We are far more contented when living out of our spirit. Also, joy will often have great expression in our lives.

Sometimes we have experienced traumas that create a situation of our soul not trusting our spirit. The soul blames the spirit for not protecting it. The irony is that typically our soul never gave place to the spirit so it could protect us. The soul places false blame on the spirit, and must be coerced to forgive the spirit, and the soul must relinquish control to the spirit. Once the soul forgives the spirit, the two components can begin to work in harmony.

If I were to flash an image of some delicious, freshly cooked donuts in front of you, what would happen? For many, their body would announce a craving for one. What if, instead, I showed you an image of a bowl of broccoli? How many people would get excited about that? Probably not as much excitement over a bowl of broccoli would be exhibited. Which does your body prefer? The donuts or the broccoli? For the untamed soul, the donuts are likely to win out every time. Which do most kids prefer?

In any case, you can train yourself to go for the healthier option. A principle regarding this that I heard years ago is summed up like this:

*What you feed will live –
what you starve will die*

What do we want to be dominant? Our spirit, our soul, or our body? The part we feed is the part that will dominate.

For some, they feed their soul and live by the logic of their mind. Everything must be reasoned out in their mind before they will accept it. However, because our soul gains its insight from the Tree of the Knowledge of Good and Evil, it will always have faulty and limited understandings.

How do we change this soul dominant or body dominant pattern? We instruct our soul to back up and we call our spirit to come forward. Some people may need to physically stand up and speak to your soul and say, "Soul, back up," and as they say those words, take a physical step backward. Then, speak to their spirit out loud and say, "Spirit, come forward." As you speak those words, take a physical step forward. This prophetic act helps trigger a shift within them.

Live spirit first!

Benefits of Living Spirit First

Why would you want to live spirit first? Let me present several reasons to you. Living spirit first will create in you an increased awareness of Heaven and the realms of Heaven. It will create a deeper comprehension of the presence of Holy Spirit, and of angels and men and women in white linen. You will be able to better hear the voice of Heaven. You will experience greater creativity, productivity, hope, and peace. You will become more aware of the needs of people that you can meet.

As you live spirit first, you will be able to access the riches of Heaven in your life. As a business owner, you will be able to engage more fully with the Business Complex of Heaven, and you will live a more fulfilling life. Petty things that formerly bothered you will dissipate in importance or impact in your life. You will be able to move ahead, not concerning yourself with the petty, mundane, or unproductive things that have affected your life before you began to live spirit first.

This way of life is more than a game changer—for the believer, it is the only way to live. You will face challenges as you build your business—or your life—from Heaven down; however, but you will more readily be able to access the solutions of Heaven as you live with an awareness of the richness of Heaven and all that is available to you as a son or daughter of the Lord Most High. I encourage you, do not live dominated by your soul. *Live spirit first!*

Four Keys to Hearing God's Voice

Dr. Mark Virkler has written extensively on this subject over the years. It is his signature teaching, and he has helped thousands of believers learn to hear and record what Heaven is saying to them on an ongoing basis. His website (cwgministries.org) has a myriad of materials to assist you in learning to do spirit-led journaling. I will simply summarize his teaching here because it is a vital discipline for you to learn to maximize Heaven down in your life.

1. **Quiet yourself** – Learn to quiet yourself so you can tune into Heaven.
2. **Look unto Jesus** – we are not looking for anyone outside of Heaven to be speaking to us—they are not invited to the party!
3. **Tune to the Flow of the Spirit Within** – The Holy Spirit flows through our spirit like a river. We can learn to tune to that flow and hear what Heaven is saying.
4. **Write it down!** —Begin to record what you are hearing or perceiving. YOU can judge it when you are finished listening for Heaven. Do not concern yourself with how it looks on the page.

Just record it—whether handwritten, drawn, or typed, make a record of it!

At CourtsNet.com you will find our video course to help you in this process.

Appendix B

Index of Types of Angels

Angels of Ambush (Ambushers) 107, 108

Angel of Currency (Currency Angel)................. 103, 104

Angels of Harvest.. 76

Angels of Healing... 40, 76

Angel of Relationships.. 104

Angels of Warfare (See Warrior Angels)

Appointed Angels.. 19

Archangels... 19

Bond Registry Angels.............................88, 97, 121-126

Bounty Hunter Angels 107, 108

Commanding Angel 25, 105

Courier Angels (See Messenger Angels)

Fallen Angels.. 9

Fire Starters.. 107, 108

Gathering Angels 9-11, 29, 76, 104

Guardian Angels 9-11, 12, 25 27-29,
.... 33, 34, 36, 37, 76 124, 126

Messenger Angels (Message Angels)...................... 9, 76
.............................89-95, 97, 99, 101, 102, 130, 172

Personal Angels..................ix, 3, 7, 9, 25, 26, 71-73, 75-77,
...................................95-100, 123-126, 145,172

Rogue Guardian Angels 28, 34

Scribe (Scribing) Angels.. 68, 169

Sent Angels 19

Sentry Angels 153

Sniper Angels 107, 108

Taxing Angels... 144-146, 149

Warring Angels (Warrior Angels)............ 12, 72, 76, 104,
....107-108, 110, 113

Index of Courts

Court of Accounting (aka Court of Proving) 143
.... 146-148, 150-152
Court of Accounting of the Words of the Saints 153
Court of Accounting of the Works of Darkness 152
Court of Accusation (Court of Hell) 107
Court of Angels 5, 73, 79, 107, 109-112
Court of Decrees 107-109, 111, 112, 114
Court of Hell 107
Court of Praise 155
Court of Reclamation 116, 143, 145-148
Court of Records 107, 122
Court of Storehouse 150
Court of Subtraction 150
Court of Tabulations 150
Court of the Adjudication of Angelic Forces
(Adjudication Court of Angels) 28, 33-35, 75
Court of Titles & Deeds 16, 180
Mercy Court 173

Description

Significant misinformation exists concerning angels, not only in the Body of Christ, but throughout the earth. We have been taught that angels are frail, dainty, cupid-like creatures that have little power and that we are subordinate to them. That is not the case.

The angels the Bible demonstrates are mighty and powerful with great strength to defeat our enemies. They appear throughout scripture to subdue kings and kingdoms, bring messages of hope, and save lives. Hebrews refers to them as ministers to those who are heirs of salvation.[36] The psalmist recorded that they were flames of fire[37]—hardly a cupid-like figure.

This book will help you learn to engage with angels, to know your Personal Angel, to understand realms, to set your angel in place to guard your realms, and much more. You will want the information in this book. It is life changing!

---

[36] Hebrews 1:14 Are they not all ministering spirits sent forth to minister for those who will inherit salvation?
[37] Psalms 104:4 Who makes His angels spirits, His ministers a flame of fire.

About the Author

Dr. Ron Horner is a communicator and author of twenty books on the subjects of the Courts of Heaven and engaging the realms of Heaven. He teaches through weekly classes, a training program, seminars, and conferences.

Ron is the founder of LifeSpring International Ministries, which serves to advocate for both individuals and businesses in the Courts of Heaven. He is also the founder of Business Advocate Services, a worldwide consulting company (BASGlobal.net).

Other Books by Dr. Ron M. Horner

Building Your Business from Heaven Down

Building Your Business from Heaven Down 2.0

Cooperating with The Glory

Engaging Angels in the Realms of Heaven

Engaging Heaven for Revelation – Volume 1

Engaging the Courts for Ownership & Order

Engaging the Courts for Your City (Paperback, Leader's Guide & Workbook)

Engaging the Courts of Healing & the Healing Garden

Engaging the Courts of Heaven

Engaging the Help Desk of the Courts of Heaven

Engaging the Mercy Court of Heaven

Four Keys to Dismantling Accusations

Freedom from Mithraism

Let's Get it Right!

Lingering Human Spirits

Overcoming the False Verdicts of Freemasonry

Overcoming Verdicts from the Courts of Hell

Releasing Bonds from the Courts of Heaven

The Courts of Heaven Process Charts

Unlocking Spiritual Seeing